ART MASTERS

THE IMPRESSIONISTS

Francesco Salvi

◆

Illustrated by
L.R. Galante & Andrea Ricciardi

THE OLIVER PRESS, INC.
MINNEAPOLIS

Produced by
Donati-Giudici Associati, Firenze
Original title
Gli impressionisti
Text
Francesco Salvi
Illustrations
L.R. Galante
Andrea Ricciardi
Editorial coordination
Francesco Fiorentino
Teresa Domenici
Francesca Romei
Art direction and design
Oliviero Ciriaci
Research
Francesca Donati
Editing
Enza Fontana
Pagination
Monica Macchiaioli
Desktop publishing
Ugo Micheli
English translation
Susan Ashley
Editor, English-language edition
Susan Ashley
Cover design
Icon Productions

Original edition copyright © 1994
Donati Giudici Associati s.r.l.
Firenze, Italia

© 2008 by VoLo publisher srl,
Firenze, Italia

This edition © 2008 by
The Oliver Press, Inc.
5707 West 36th Street
Minneapolis, MN 55416
United States of America
www.oliverpress.com

Publisher Cataloging Data

Salvi, Francesco
        The impressionists / Francesco
Salvi ; illustrated by L.R. Galante & Andrea
Ricciardi ; [English translation, Susan
Ashley].
        p. cm. – (Art masters)
        Includes bibliographical
references and index.
        Summary: This book describes
the development of Impressionism and
presents the eleven artists who made up
the Impressionist group, including
reproductions and analyses of
their work.
        ISBN 978-1-934545-03-4
        1. Impressionism (Art)–Juvenile
literature 2. Art, Modern–19th century–
Juvenile literature [1. Impressionism
(Art) 2. Art Modern–19th century
3. Art appreciation] I. Galante, L. R.
II. Ricciardi, Andrea III. Ashley, Susan
IV. Title V. Series
        2008
        759.05'4–dc22

ISBN 978-1-934545-03-4

Printed in Italy

11 10 09 08   4 3 2 1

♦ How to Use This Book

Each double-page spread is a chapter in its own right, devoted to a key theme in the development of Impressionism. The theme is introduced in the paragraph at the top of the left-hand page and depicted in the large, central illustration. The second paragaph on the spread gives a chronological account of the artists' lives. The smaller text and illustrations on each spread expand on the central theme.

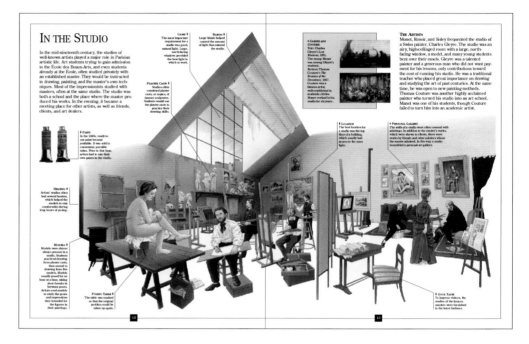

Pages 46 through 61 present the eleven artists who made up the Impressionist group. Each section includes a biography of the artist in the left-hand column and an overview of the artist's style at the top of the page. A major work by the artist is reproduced in the center of the page, with an analysis of the work in the paragraph below. Each section offers further examination of the work in the form of detailed close-ups, as well as additional examples of the artists' work.

CONTENTS

THE CHARACTERS

Looking at Impressionist paintings today, with their pleasing colors and engaging subject matter, it is hard to imagine they were once considered radical, even obscene. When viewed in the context of the nineteenth century, however, the paintings were revolutionary. At the beginning of the century, the prevailing view of art was that it should depict historical or religious themes and treat them dramatically —with deep shadows, artificial lighting, and figures that were so idealized, they didn't seem human. The Impressionists challenged this traditional definition of art. They went outside and painted the world around them, whether it was the modern boulevards of Paris or a stand of trees along a river. It wasn't just their subject matter that was new, but the way in which they depicted it. They used bright colors and applied them to the canvas in rough dabs of paint. Critics accused them of using a sloppy technique and trivial subject matter, but the Impressionists persevered. They were young men and women who, despite their diverse backgrounds, were united in their quest to establish a new style of painting.

✦ **PAUL DURAND-RUEL**
Durand-Ruel was a French art dealer and the Impressionists' greatest advocate. He created a market for their work throughout Europe and also in the United States.

✦ **THE HAVEMEYERS**
Friends of the painter Mary Cassatt, Henry and Louisine Havemeyer were the leading collectors of Impressionist art in America.

✦ **FÉLIX NADAR**
A pioneering French photographer, Nadar was a friend of the Impressionists and lent them his studio for their first exhibition.

✦ **GUSTAVE CAILLEBOTTE**
Caillebotte had many interests in addition to painting and used his wealth to help support his fellow Impressionists.

✦ **BERTHE MORISOT**
A close friend of Manet, Morisot was the first female to exhibit with the Impressionists.

✦ **ARMAND GUILLAUMIN**
Known for his bold colors, Guillaumin sometimes painted scenes of the grittier, industrial sections of the modern city.

MARY CASSATT ✦
Cassatt was an American who moved to Paris and joined the Impressionists. She was influenced by Japanese art.

✦ **Napoleon III**
Nephew of Napoleon Bonaparte, he took power in 1851 and was the leader of France until 1870. He hired Haussmann to modernize Paris.

✦ **Baron Haussmann**
A civic planner who, in the 1860s, transformed Paris from a medieval city into an elegant, modern metropolis.

✦ **Émile Zola**
A writer and journalist, Zola defended the Impressionists when art critics attacked their work.

✦ **Jurymen of the Salon**
The Salon was an annual art exhibition in Paris. A conservative jury determined whose work would be shown.

✦ **Gustave Courbet**
The founder of Realism, an art movement in the mid-nineteenth century that rejected the idealistic art of the past.

✦ **Louis Leroy**
An art critic who coined the term "Impressionism" as a slight to the artists.

✦ **Paul Cézanne**
A native of Provence, Cézanne experimented with Impressionist techniques, but later developed his own unique style.

✦ **Alfred Sisley**
Born in Paris to an English family, Sisley is known for his landscapes and scenes of rural towns outside of Paris.

✦ **Claude Monet**
A leader of the Impressionist movement, Monet painted well into his eighties. His canvases reflect his fascination with light.

✦ **Edgar Degas**
Known best for his scenes of the ballet, Degas worked in pastels as well as oils, and later turned to sculpture.

✦ **Pierre-Auguste Renoir**
Renoir is known for his scenes of young Parisians enjoying themselves at fashionable meeting spots.

✦ **Camille Pissarro**
The eldest of the Impressionists, Pissarro was also a mentor to many of the younger artists in the group.

✦ **Édouard Manet**
Manet's work forms a bridge between the Realist movement of the mid-nineteenth century and Impressionism.

THE SITES

The city of Paris is central to the story of Impressionism. Paris was the hub of the Western art world in the nineteenth century. It had the most prestigious art schools and attracted the most talented artists. The painters who became the Impressionists came to Paris to study. They lived and worked in the city, and held their first exhibitions there. Paris itself became the subject of many of their paintings: the Batignolles quarter where many had their studios; the Louvre where they studied artists of the past; the broad new avenues, parks, and railroad stations; the Moulin Rouge and other cafés where they socialized. The city offered an endless range of subjects to paint. Beyond Paris, the Impressionists captured landscapes, rural towns along the Seine River, and resorts on the Atlantic seacoast. During the Franco-Prussian War in 1870–1871, London became the subject of Impressionist paintings when Monet and Pissarro took refuge in the city.

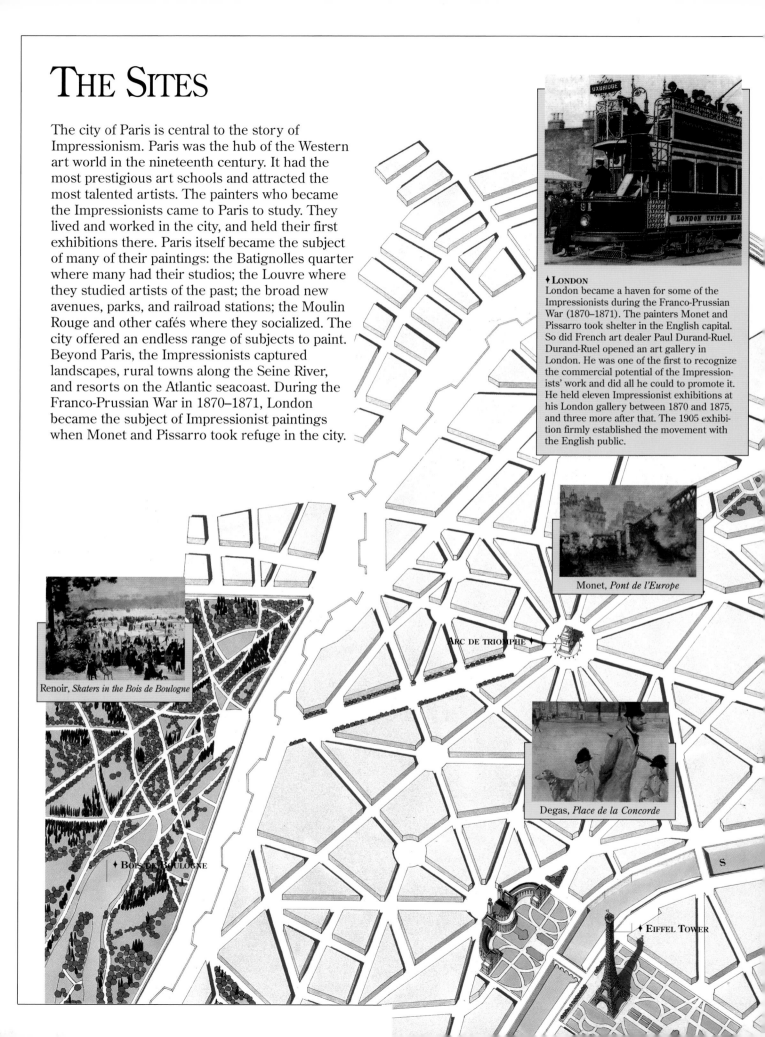

♦ LONDON
London became a haven for some of the Impressionists during the Franco-Prussian War (1870–1871). The painters Monet and Pissarro took shelter in the English capital. So did French art dealer Paul Durand-Ruel. Durand-Ruel opened an art gallery in London. He was one of the first to recognize the commercial potential of the Impressionists' work and did all he could to promote it. He held eleven Impressionist exhibitions at his London gallery between 1870 and 1875, and three more after that. The 1905 exhibition firmly established the movement with the English public.

Monet, *Pont de l'Europe*

Renoir, *Skaters in the Bois de Boulogne*

Degas, *Place de la Concorde*

ARC DE TRIOMPHE ♦

♦ BOIS DE BOULOGNE

S

♦ EIFFEL TOWER

Renoir, *Moulin de la Galette*

Sisley, *View of Montmartre*

♦ **NEW YORK**
Art dearler Durand-Ruel was responsible for introducing Impressionism to the United States. He held a large exhibition in New York in 1886 and opened an art gallery on Fifth Avenue. Not all of the Impressionists were happy to send their work to the American market. Monet, for example, maintained that good taste was only to be found in Paris and Americans could not appreciate his painting. Any objections were soon withdrawn, however, when Americans greeted the new art with enthusiasm and brought some of the painters their first financial success.

BATIGNOLLES ♦

Monet, *Gare Saint-Lazare*

SACRÉ COEUR

♦ MOULIN DE LA GALETTE

♦ MOULIN ROUGE

♦ CAFÉ GUERBOIS

♦ PARC MONCEAU

GARE SAINT-LAZARE ♦

Pissarro, *Avenue de l'Opéra*

Pissarro, *Boulevard des Italiens*

♦ OPÉRA

Monet, *Boulevard des Capucines*

♦ PLACE VENDÔME

♦ PALAIS DE L'INDUSTRIE

LOUVRE

♦ LES HALLES

Guillaumin, *Bridge of Louis Philippe*

N E

HÔTEL DE VILLE ♦

NOTRE-DAME ♦

ÉCOLE DES BEAUX-ARTS

Monet, *Les Tuileries*

Monet, *Quai du Louvre*

THE NEW PARIS

♦ PUBLIC TOILETS
Public toilets were
another innovation
in the redesign
of Paris.

Between 1800 and 1850, the population of Paris
doubled, growing from 500,000 to one million.
The city's residents were crowded into the old
medieval town center where sanitary conditions
were poor. Napoleon III, the last French monarch,
ordered a radical redevelopment of the city. He
employed Baron Haussmann, a French city planner, to do the job. Between 1853 and 1870, the
city of Paris was transformed. Entire neighbor-
hoods were demolished, and the narrow medieval
streets were replaced by broad, tree-lined boulevards. Haussmann designed grand public spaces
and constructed over 40,000 new buildings. The
new Paris was modern and sophisticated. The
Impressionists were inspired by this new urban
setting and began documenting it on canvas.

♦ **HAUSSMANN AND
NAPOLEON III**
Haussmann's name
is synonymous with
the rebuilding of
Paris, but his work
would not have been
possible without the
will and determina-
tion of Napoleon III.
In 1850, central Paris
was an area of
narrow streets and
slums. Napoleon III
ordered a modern-
ization of the city,
which meant
demolishing many
of the older districts.
He also moved
working-class neigh-
borhoods to the
outskirts of the city.

♦ **URBAN DESIGN**
Haussmann's plans
included columns
like the one above.
The columns held
posters and
advertisements.

♦ **THE OPPONENTS**
Many people were
unhappy with
Haussmann's
transformation of
Paris. One opponent
of the new Paris was
Victor Hugo (shown
above), the great
nineteenth-century
French novelist and
author of *Les
Misérables*.
Haussmann was
blamed for the
excessive cost of
the reconstruction,
the sometimes
unnecessary
demolition of ancient
buildings, and the
social unrest caused
by creating a new
city center for the
wealthy, while the
working classes
were moved to
outlying suburbs.

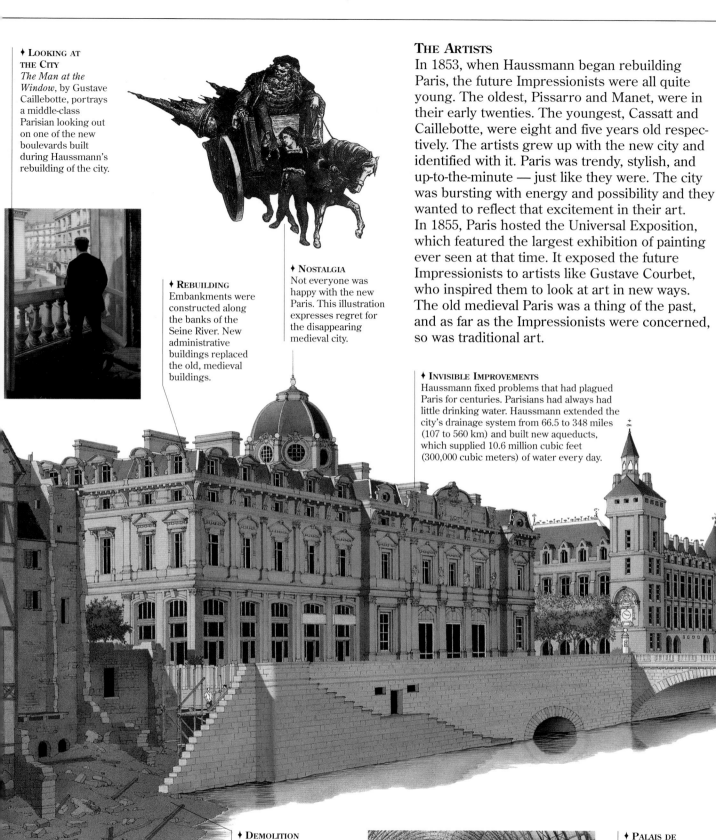

♦ LOOKING AT THE CITY
The Man at the Window, by Gustave Caillebotte, portrays a middle-class Parisian looking out on one of the new boulevards built during Haussmann's rebuilding of the city.

♦ REBUILDING
Embankments were constructed along the banks of the Seine River. New administrative buildings replaced the old, medieval buildings.

♦ NOSTALGIA
Not everyone was happy with the new Paris. This illustration expresses regret for the disappearing medieval city.

THE ARTISTS

In 1853, when Haussmann began rebuilding Paris, the future Impressionists were all quite young. The oldest, Pissarro and Manet, were in their early twenties. The youngest, Cassatt and Caillebotte, were eight and five years old respectively. The artists grew up with the new city and identified with it. Paris was trendy, stylish, and up-to-the-minute — just like they were. The city was bursting with energy and possibility and they wanted to reflect that excitement in their art. In 1855, Paris hosted the Universal Exposition, which featured the largest exhibition of painting ever seen at that time. It exposed the future Impressionists to artists like Gustave Courbet, who inspired them to look at art in new ways. The old medieval Paris was a thing of the past, and as far as the Impressionists were concerned, so was traditional art.

♦ INVISIBLE IMPROVEMENTS
Haussmann fixed problems that had plagued Paris for centuries. Parisians had always had little drinking water. Haussmann extended the city's drainage system from 66.5 to 348 miles (107 to 560 km) and built new aqueducts, which supplied 10.6 million cubic feet (300,000 cubic meters) of water every day.

♦ DEMOLITION
The heart of medieval Paris lay between the cathedral of Notre Dame and the old Palais Royal. It had become a meeting place for thieves and was a dangerous part of the city.

♦ PALAIS DE L'INDUSTRIE
The Palais was an enormous metal and glass structure built for the Universal Exposition, or World's Fair, of 1855. Later, it housed the prestigious painting Salons.

EARLY TRAINING

In their youth, the future Impressionist painters often visited the Louvre Museum in the heart of Paris. There, they could view masterpieces of Italian, French, Flemish, and Spanish art and copy paintings by the old masters. Studying and copying great works from previous centuries was considered essential training for young artists. Some of the future Impressionists attended the École des Beaux-Arts (School of Fine Arts) in Paris. Monet, Renoir, and Degas studied there. Women were not admitted to the school until 1897. The École was extremely traditional and urged students to look to the past for inspiration and technique.

✦ **DEGAS AND INGRES**
Far left: Jean Auguste Dominique Ingres, *The Bather of Valpinçon*, 1808 (The Louvre, Paris) Left: *The Bather,* Edgar Degas, 1855 This sketch reflects Degas's admiration for Ingres. Degas viewed Ingres as a master of drawing and composition.

Antoine Watteau ✦
(1684-1721)

Hans Holbein ✦
(1497-1543)

Rembrandt van Rijn ✦
(1606-1668)

François Boucher ✦
(1703-1770)

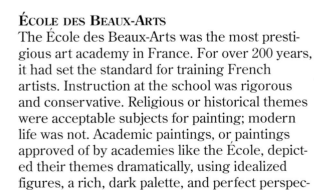

✦ **MASTERS AND PUPILS**
At the Louvre, Renoir was attracted to eighteenth-century masters like Watteau and Boucher. Monet preferred Rembrandt and the Spanish masters. Degas made copies of Holbein, Delacroix, and Ingres.

ÉCOLE DES BEAUX-ARTS

The École des Beaux-Arts was the most prestigious art academy in France. For over 200 years, it had set the standard for training French artists. Instruction at the school was rigorous and conservative. Religious or historical themes were acceptable subjects for painting; modern life was not. Academic paintings, or paintings approved of by academies like the École, depicted their themes dramatically, using idealized figures, a rich, dark palette, and perfect perspective. Academic paintings had a smooth surface in which the artist's brushstrokes were not visible. The Impressionists would break with this traditional interpretation of art.

♦ **Jusepe de Ribera**
(1591-1652)

Eugène Delacroix ♦
(1798-1863)

♦ **THE LOUVRE**
The Louvre Museum
is one of the oldest
and largest
museums in the
world. It opened to
the public in 1793.
Napoleon III added
to its collection of
new works.

IN THE STUDIO

In the mid-nineteenth century, the studios of well-known artists played a major role in Parisian artistic life. Art students trying to gain admission to the École des Beaux-Arts, and even students already at the École, often studied privately with an established master. They would be instructed in drawing, painting, and the master's own techniques. Most of the Impressionists studied with masters, often at the same studio. The studio was both a school and the place where the master produced his works. In the evening, it became a meeting place for other artists, as well as friends, clients, and art dealers.

LIGHT ✦
The most important requirement for a studio was good, natural light. Large, north-facing windows provided the best light in which to work.

BLINDS ✦
Large blinds helped control the amount of light that entered the studio.

PLASTER CASTS ✦
Studios often contained plaster casts, or copies, of famous sculptures. Students would use the plaster casts to practice their drawing skills.

✦ PAINT
In the 1840s, ready-to-use paint became available. It was sold in convenient, portable tubes. Prior to that time, artists had to mix their own paints in the studio.

HEATING ✦
Artists' studios often had several heaters, which helped the models to stay comfortable during long hours of posing.

MODELS ✦
Models were almost always present in a studio. Students practiced drawing from plaster casts, then moved to drawing from live models. Models usually posed for an hour at a time, taking short breaks in between poses. Artists used models to study the poses and expressions they intended for the figures in their paintings.

POSING TABLE ✦
The table was marked so that the original position could be taken up again.

Top: Charles Gleyre's *Lost Illusions,* 1851. The young Monet was among Gleyre's students. Bottom: Thomas Couture's *The Romans of the Decadence,* 1847. Couture was a famous artist, well-established in academic circles. Manet worked in his studio for six years .

THE ARTISTS

Monet, Renoir, and Sisley frequented the studio of a Swiss painter, Charles Gleyre. The studio was an airy, high-ceilinged room with a large, north-facing window, a model, and many young students bent over their easels. Gleyre was a talented painter and a generous man who did not want payment for his lessons, only contributions toward the cost of running his studio. He was a traditional teacher who placed great importance on drawing and studying the art of past centuries. At the same time, he was open to new painting methods. Thomas Couture was another highly acclaimed painter who turned his studio into an art school. Manet was one of his students, though Couture failed to turn him into an academic artist.

♦ LOCATION
The best location for a studio was the top floor of a building, which usually had access to the most light.

♦ PERSONAL GALLERY
The walls of a studio were often covered with paintings. In addition to the master's works, which were shown to clients, there were works by friends and other painters whom the master admired. In this way, a studio resembled a personal art gallery.

♦ GOOD TASTE
To impress visitors, the studios of the famous masters were furnished in the latest fashions.

THE MASTERS OF REALISM

In the mid-nineteenth century, a new movement called Realism changed French painting. Led by Gustav Courbet, the artists in this new style rebelled against the idealized subject matter of the past. They were not interested in painting beautiful pictures or historical scenes. Their goal was to portray the life around them as honestly as possible. For the first time, ordinary workers and peasants became the focus of paintings. The Realists did not hesitate to show the harsher side of life and often used dark, somber colors appropriate to their subject matter. The Realists caused a great scandal in academic circles. The elimination of Greek gods and religious figures from their paintings was shocking. The Impressionists, however, were inspired. They, too, wanted to depict everyday life, but in their own way.

✦ AGAINST TRADITION
After his paintings were rejected by the jury of the Paris Universal Exposition in 1855, Gustave Courbet (1819–1877) built his own pavillion, next-door, where he exhbitied fifty paintings. It was the first sign of a break with tradition.

REALISTS ✦ AND ACADEMICS
A cartoon by Honoré Daumier (1808–1879) illustrates the clash between the two schools. The Realist (left) wears working-class clothes.

✦ GUSTAVE COURBET
A photograph of the master of Realism, taken around 1850.

✦ PALETTE KNIVES
Traditionally, artists used palette knives (middle) to mix colors on the palette (right). Realist painters, and later the Impressionists, began using them to apply paint to the canvas.

✦ COURBET'S STUDIO
The title of this painting by Gustave Courbet is *The painter's studio, a real allegory summing up seven years in my artistic life*. Courbet is in the middle, seated at his easel. Next to him is a child, a symbol of innocence. To the left are representatives of the working classes; on the right, writers and intellectuals. Courbet said the painting showed "all the people who serve my cause, sustain me in my ideal and support my activity (creating art)." The painting was one of the two rejected by the Exposition in 1855.

✦ **Corot Outdoors**
A picture of the aged Jean-Baptiste-Camille Corot (1796–1875) following the Impressionist example and painting outdoors. Corot came into contact with Impressionist techniques late in life and believed that a landscape begun outdoors should be finished with accuracy in the studio.

The Artists

French painter Gustave Courbet coined the term "Realism" to describe the new art movement. He believed a painting should capture its subject truthfully, with no embellishment. Courbet was passionate about social issues and his paintings often depicted the grim working conditions of the poor. Jean-François Millet, another Realist painter, also depicted the working classes. His paintings of peasants were an inspiration to many artists. In traditional painting, peasants, if they appeared at all, were always in the background. In Millet's work, peasants are the central focus and their work is seen as noble. The Impressionists shared the Realists' interest in depicting everyday life, but their palettes would become much brighter and their compositions less formal than those of the Realists.

✦ **An Inspiration**
Left: Corot, *View of Ville d'Avray*
Corot's luminous landscapes, with their warm, natural light, were admired by the Impressionists.

✦ **Courbet's Shocking Painting**
Courbet's *The Burial at Ornans* was exhibited at the 1851 Salon. The painting caused a scandal because it depicted an ordinary funeral and the people who attended it just as they were, with no embellishment.

✦ **Millet's Peasants**
Right: *The Gleaners*, painted by Jean-François Millet (1814–1875) in 1857. Millet's portrayal of peasants working in the fields became an inspiration to many painters. It was the first time that peasants became fully accepted as a subject for painting. In 1848, disgusted by city life, which he believed to be alienating and inhuman, Millet moved to Barbizon, a country town southeast of Paris, where he spent the rest of his life.

IN THE OPEN AIR

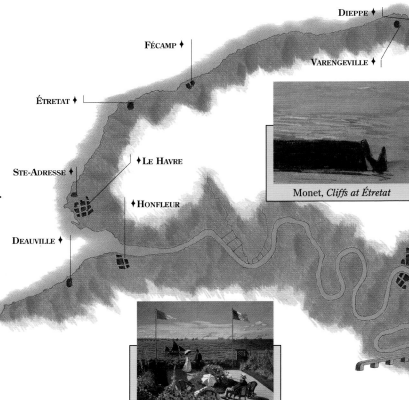

The Impressionists broke many rules of academic painting. One was their insistence on working direct from experience. For them, painting did not mean staying behind closed doors in the cold light of a studio, but taking easel, canvas, and paints and working *en plein air* (outdoors). This gave their canvases a feeling of spontaneity, but it also required some new painting techniques. Outdoors, light is constantly changing, and an artist has to be quick to capture it. The Impressionists learned to use short, rapid brushstrokes. They didn't bother with outlines or details; a few dabs of color could suggest an entire field of flowers.

DIEPPE

FÉCAMP

VARENGEVILLE

ÉTRETAT

STE-ADRESSE

LE HAVRE

HONFLEUR

DEAUVILLE

Monet, *Cliffs at Étretat*

Monet, *Terrace at Sainte-Adresse*

✦ THE TRAIN
The new railway lines leading to and from Paris allowed the Impressionists to travel to small towns and the countryside beyond the city to paint.

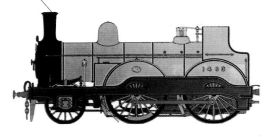

Monet, *The Artist's Garden at Giverny*

Pissarro, *Rue de l'Épicerie, Rouen*

THE ARTISTS

Several factors, beyond a quick painting technique, helped make painting *en plein air* feasible for the Impressionists. One was the invention of ready-to-use paints. Before the 1840s, painters had to mix their own paints with pigments and oil. The new paints came in convenient tubes, making them very portable. More importantly, the railroad arrived in France in the second half of the nineteenth century. The first lines connected Paris to outlying towns and cities. Now Parisians could commute to other parts of France in a matter of hours. Along with the railroad came the development of new resorts. Many were on the Atlantic coast. The Impressionists took advantage of the new railway system to paint a variety of new subjects: the countryside, the seacoast, and towns beyond Paris.

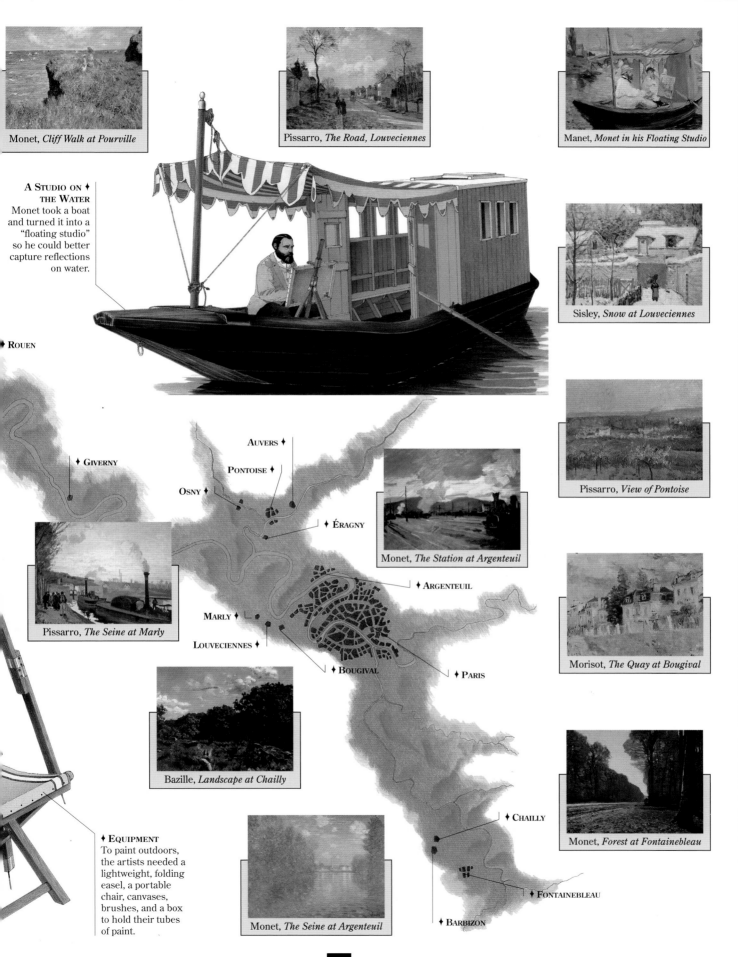

Monet, *Cliff Walk at Pourville*

Pissarro, *The Road, Louveciennes*

Manet, *Monet in his Floating Studio*

A STUDIO ON ✦ THE WATER
Monet took a boat and turned it into a "floating studio" so he could better capture reflections on water.

✦ ROUEN

Sisley, *Snow at Louveciennes*

Pissarro, *View of Pontoise*

AUVERS ✦

PONTOISE ✦

OSNY ✦

✦ GIVERNY

✦ ÉRAGNY

Monet, *The Station at Argenteuil*

✦ ARGENTEUIL

Pissarro, *The Seine at Marly*

MARLY ✦

Morisot, *The Quay at Bougival*

LOUVECIENNES ✦

✦ BOUGIVAL   ✦ PARIS

Bazille, *Landscape at Chailly*

✦ CHAILLY

Monet, *Forest at Fontainebleau*

✦ EQUIPMENT
To paint outdoors, the artists needed a lightweight, folding easel, a portable chair, canvases, brushes, and a box to hold their tubes of paint.

Monet, *The Seine at Argenteuil*

✦ FONTAINEBLEAU

✦ BARBIZON

NATURE

Nature had appeared in art before the time of the Impressionists. In academic painting, however, it was merely a backdrop for the picture's main theme. In the hands of the Impressionists, nature itself became the theme. The Impressionists were inspired by a group of French landscape painters known as the Barbizon school. The Barbizon artists were part of the Realist movement. They believed in working directly from nature and were the first to paint landscapes outdoors. The Impressionists painted landscapes in all seasons and at all times of the day. Their canvases were full of movement: clouds racing across the sky, leaves rustling on a tree, a flag flapping in the breeze. They were also full of light, reflecting the bright heat of a summer day or the crisp coolness of a winter morning. The academics had never held landscape painting in high regard, but the Impressionists raised it to a prominence that it still holds today.

♦ BEECH TREES
A forest of beech trees in the fall, by the German photographer Albert Renger-Patzsch.

COUNTRYSIDE ♦
Except for Degas, the Impressionists enjoyed painting landscapes and spent a great deal of time in the countryside. Their techniques were ideal for capturing nature's changing light and colors.

1. Sisley, *Wheatfields near Argenteuil*
2. Renoir, *Path Climbing Through Long Grass*

SKY ♦
Impressionist skies are never just a background, but are filled with light and movement. With a few quick brushstrokes, the Impressionists were able to suggest the puffy clouds of a summer sky or an oncoming rainstorm.

1. Renoir, *Gust of Wind*
2. Cézanne, *The Seine at Bercy*
3. Guillaumin, *The Seine at Charenton*
4. Pissarro, *February Sunrise*

THE SEA ♦
Water is a feature in many Impressionist paintings. The artists were fascinated by its changing colors and the reflection of sunlight on water. Many of their paintings portrayed life at seaside resorts, which were very popular in the late nineteenth century.

1. Manet, *Rochefort's Escape*
2. Monet, *Terrace at Sainte-Adresse*

2

TREES ♦

Trees and woods became a subject of Impressionist paintings. Trees offered endless variety in terms of form, foliage, and color, and their branches and leaves were full of movement. Monet, in particular, produced a famous series on poplars, portraying their tall, graceful trunks in different light conditions.

1. Monet, *Poplars*
2. Cézanne, *Wood in Provence*

1

2

3

4

SNOW ♦

The Impressionists were interested in snow because of its ability to reflect light. For them, snow was full of color. Shadows on snow, in particular, were a range of deep blues. Snow also transformed the shapes of ordinary things and allowed the artists to depict trees, fields, and fences in new ways.

Monet, *The Magpie*

2

STILL LIFE ♦

Not all of the Impressionists regularly applied themselves to still life, one of the traditional subjects of painting. Paul Cézanne is the artist most associated with it. Nearly all of his still lifes include fruit, which allowed him to study the colors and shapes of everyday things.

1. Cézanne, *Still Life with Apples and Biscuits*
2. Manet, *Roses and Tulips in a Dragon Vase*

1

2

THE SALON

The Salon was an annual juried exhibition of artwork in Paris. Its influence in the French art world was so great that painters chosen to exhibit were almost guaranteed of success, while those rejected had little chance of selling their work. The jury favored traditional, academic painting and often refused work that was unconventional. In 1863, the jury rejected over 2,000 paintings, an unusually high number. Artists accused the jury of being biased and caused such an uproar that Napoleon III intervened. He went to see the rejected paintings and ordered a separate exhibition to be set up, called the *Salon des Refusés* (Salon of the Refused). It opened in May 1863. Public opinion and professional criticism were severe, but at least the rejected artists were able to exhibit their work.

THE SALON BUILDING ✦
During the second half of the nineteenth century, the Salon was held in the Palais de l'Industrie, a metal and glass exhibition hall that had been built for the 1855 Universal Exposition in Paris.

THE ARTISTS

Although they rebelled against tradition, many Impressionists continued to submit works to the Salon jury in the hope of being accepted. It was an artist's best chance to gain recognition — and to make a living. Most of their works were rejected. For others, success alternated with rejection. Manet received an honorable mention in 1861, but his painting *Luncheon on the Grass* was rejected in 1863. He was able to show it at the Salon des Réfuses, but the critics condemned it.

THE ARRIVAL ✦ OF NAPOLEON
Napoleon III visited the Salon when he learned about the thousands of works that had been rejected. He ordered them to be shown in a separate exhibition called the Salon des Refusés.

♦ **TOO MANY WORKS**
The exhibition hall on the eve of the opening of the 1863 Salon. That year, over half of the works submitted had been rejected — for lack of space, if not style.

♦ **SHOCKING WORKS**
Luncheon on the Grass (top) and *Olympia* (bottom) were two of Manet's paintings that shocked the public and critics. The first was rejected by the 1863 Salon and shown at the Salon des Refusés. The second, accepted by the 1865 Salon, was met with scorn from art critics. Traditionally, nude figures were acceptable only when depicting mythological characters.

♦ **DISPLAYING THE ART**
Nearly every inch of space was used to display the art. Paintings were placed one on top of the other, all the way up to the ceiling.

JAPANESE ART

The Universal Exposition, or World's Fair, held in Paris in 1867 featured products and crafts from around the world. For artists who attended the fair, one country's products stood out among all the rest: Japan. The exposition was the first time most Westerners had ever seen Japanese art. The Impressionists, in particular, were fascinated. They admired the simplicity, asymmetrical composition, and pure, bright colors found in Japanese prints. There was also an absence of shadows, which gave the prints a flat, two-dimensional look. Many of these techniques found their way into Impressionist paintings. European artists also began using Japanese objects as props in their paintings, including fans, vases, and kimonos.

✦ HOKUSAI
Above: A self-portrait of Hokusai at the age of eighty. Hokusai (1760–1849) was a painter and printmaker who became one of the most famous and influential Japanese artists of the nineteenth century. He was active as a painter for over seventy years and created an incredible number of prints on many different themes, including landscapes, portraits, and birds. His most famous work was *Thirty-six Views of Mount Fuji*, a series of woodblock prints produced between 1826 and 1833. This series secured his fame in the West and continues to inspire artists today, including graphic designers and cartoon illustrators.

✦ A FAN
The Impressionists were interested in all things Japanese, including fans like this one. The illustration is the work of Japanese artist Kuniyoshi.

✦ A CHANCE ENCOUNTER
Knowledge of Hokusai's work in France dated back to a chance encounter. In 1856, French painter Félix Braquemond was unwrapping some porcelain that had come from Japan. He was amazed by the paper that was used to wrap the porcelain. The sheets were pages from a book of Hokusai prints. He hurried to show them to his artist friends.

♦ **MARY CASSATT AND JAPANESE ART**
The two watercolors to the left by Mary Cassatt, *The Hairstyle* and *Women Bathing*, show how clearly the artist was inspired by Japanese prints.

MONET ♦ AND JAPAN
In 1876, Monet painted his wife wearing a kimono in a work titled *La Japonaise.*

♦ **MONET'S BRIDGE**
Monet moved to the quiet town of Giverny in 1883. There, he built a bridge over his pond (shown left in his painting *The Japanese Bridge in Giverny*) whose design was clearly inspired by bridges he had seen in Japanese prints (right).

THE ARTISTS

With the exception of Cézanne and Renoir, who were indifferent to what they considered a passing fashion, the Impressionists were captivated by Japanese art. They were frequent visitors and clients of a shop called The Chinese Door in central Paris, which displayed Asian art, including Japanese prints, fans, costumes, and other handicrafts. Degas collected Japanese prints. Monet portrayed his wife dressed in a kimono and surrounded by fans. Later, in his garden at Giverny, he had a bridge built in a Japanese style. Of all the Impressionists, however, Mary Cassatt was the artist most influenced by Japanese art.

PHOTOGRAPHY

The invention of the camera in the middle of the nineteenth century allowed photography to invade an area that was previously the preserve of painting. Photographers, as well as painters, could now produce portraits, landscapes, and city scenes. Many artists regarded the camera with suspicion and concern. The Impressionists, however, saw it as a powerful tool to study movement, gesture, and perspective. Photographs permitted them to study subjects at length and notice details that would normally escape the eye. The camera also allowed them to capture images and keep them for use at a later time. It is not surprising that the Impressionists embraced photography: the camera captured the same fleeting, real-life moments they sought to portray on canvas.

✦ FROM CAMERA OBSCURA TO PHOTOGRAPHY
A camera obscura is a portable optical device (shown above) consisting of a dark box with a hole on one side. When light passes through the hole, it projects an image of the scene in front of the camera onto the back wall of the box. A modern camera operates on a similar theory. By adding a lense and a mirror tilted at a 45-degree angle, the image could be reflected upward onto a piece of tracing paper. For centuries, artists had used the camera obscura to help them draw perfect perspective. In 1839, French artist Louis Daguerre invented a way to capture the image permanently onto a chemically treated plate. This was the beginning of modern photography.

THE PLATE ✦
The light-sensitive plate was inside a covered plate-holder. Once an image was focused on the glass screen at the back of the camera, the photographer inserted the plate in place of the screen, removed the cover, and let in light through the lens.

THE LENS ✦
The lens was in a movable tube that could be adjusted to make the image sharper.

EXPOSURE ✦
The lens cover was used to control the length of the exposure.

THE COLOR ✦ WHEEL
Chevreul designed this wheel to show relationships between colors. Those on the blue side are called "cool" colors, while those on the red side are called "warm" colors.

✦ A PHOTOGRAPH OF CHEVREUL
Félix Nadar (right), interviews Michel Eugène Chevreul (1786–1889) on the occasion of his 101st birthday. Chevreul was a French chemist whose studies of color influenced the work of many artists, including the Impressionists.

NADAR IN A ✦ BALLOOON
Félix Nadar, a famous French photographer, was the first to use a hot-air balloon for aerial photography.

♦ MOVEMENT
Eadweard James
Muybridge
(1830–1904) created
a camera to
photograph moving
figures. His book,
Animal Locomotion,
published in 1875, was
popular with artists
and helped them
understand movement.

**DEGAS ♦
AND PHOTOGRAPHY**
*After the Bath–
Woman Drying Herself.*
Degas took the
photograph above in
1896 and used it as the
basis for his painting.

♦ GLASS SCREEN
The photographer
used the glass
screen at the back of
the camera to frame
and focus the image.

♦ BELLOWS
The photographer
used the bellows to
adjust the focus.

AN EARLY SNAPSHOT ♦
A photo by Pierre Petit
shows the construc-
tion of the Statue of
Liberty, which was
built between
1876 and 1881.

PARIS FROM ABOVE ♦
Nadar took this
photograph of Paris
from a hot-air balloon.

THE ARTISTS

Paris was an important center for the study of
photography, mainly because of pioneers like
Félix Nadar, who produced numerous portraits
and city scenes during the Haussmann years.
Nadar became a friend of the Impressionists and
would later host their first exhibition. Most of the
Impressionists owned cameras — Monet had four
— and aspects of photography emerged in their
paintings. People in the background of photographs were often blurred, and Monet began
blurring some of the figures in his paintings.
Images in photos were often off-center or cropped
off at the edge. Degas, in particular, began using
these techniques in his work.

PORTRAITS

The spontaneity captured in photographs had an effect on Impressionist portrait painting. Traditional portraits were formal and posed, with a subject who looked directly at the viewer and often seemed detached from the background of the painting. Impressionist portraits were much more candid. Like snapshots, they portrayed people in their natural surroundings, going about their daily business. Often, the subjects are so wrapped up in the action of the painting, they are not even looking at the viewer. While traditional portraiture depicted royalty and wealthy or powerful people, the Impressionists painted men, women, and children of all classes — at home, at work, and at leisure. The people in their portraits are not idealized. They are real people, with unique features and distinct personalities. They live in the paintings, together with the objects and people around them.

♦ THE FIRST SNAPSHOTS
This 1886 photograph by Alfred Stieglitz shows a young portrait photographer at work.

CHILDREN ♦
The Impressionists often painted portraits of children. The world of childhood appealed to them because it offered a variety of themes, and subjects who were natural and unaccustomed to posing.

1. Degas, *The Bellelli Family*
2. Manet, *The Fifer*
3. Degas, *Hortense Valpinçon*
4. Manet, *Boy Blowing Soap Bubbles*
5. Renoir, *The Children's Afternoon at Wargemont*

THE MIDDLE ♦ CLASS
The middle class was the subject of many Impressionist paintings. The artists portrayed people at work in the city, relaxing at home, and enjoying their favorite pastimes.

1. Degas, *The Cotton Exchange, New Orleans*
2. Degas, *At the Stock Exchange*
3. Manet, *The Balcony*
4. Cassatt, *Lady at the Tea Table*
5. Renoir, *Monsieur and Madame Bernheim de Villers*

WORKERS ♦
The Impressionists also portrayed people who carried out the menial tasks required by modern city life.

1. Manet, *The Beer Waitress*
2. Pissarro, *The Pork Butcher*
3. Renoir, *Young Woman Sewing*
4. Degas, *A Woman Ironing*
5. Caillebotte, *The Floorscrapers*

PAINTING ♦ EACH OTHER

In addition to self-portraits, the Impressionists enjoyed painting each other. Manet painted his friend and colleague, Berthe Morisot, who became his sister-in-law when she married his brother Eugene. Monet and Renoir were often in each other's company, working together *en plein air* and painting the same subjects. When artists worked together, it was common for them to paint each other's portraits or portray each other in the midst of painting.

1. Degas, *Self-portrait*
2. Cézanne, *Self-portrait*
3. Manet, *Berthe Morisot in a Black Hat, with a Bunch of Violets*
4. Caillebotte, *Self-portrait*
5. Renoir, *Claude Monet Reading*

THE NUDE ♦

When painting nudes, traditional painters worked in the studio and portrayed idealized bodies in historical contexts. The Impressionists portrayed ordinary people, often in the midst of daily activities, like taking a bath. Their models often were not professional and the poses are fresh and natural.

1. Cézanne, *The Large Bathers*
2. Degas, *The Tub*
3. Renoir, *Nude in the Sunlight*
4. Renoir, *Nana*

Along the Seine

La Grenouillère (grahn wee air) was a floating restaurant and resort along the Seine River, on the outskirts of Paris. It was easily accessible by train—the first railway line built in France. Because of the railroad, Parisians could now escape the city and spend a day or a weekend in the countryside. People came to La Grenouillère to eat, swim, and take a boat out on the river. In the evening, there was dancing. The resort was very popular. Even Napoleon III and his wife made a visit in 1869. That same year, both Monet and Renoir produced paintings of La Grenouillère. Monet stayed in the area for two months in the summer of 1869. The artists' canvases capture the lively, fashionable atmosphere of the resort.

♦ THE POSTER
A poster describes the variety of entertainment Parisians would find at La Grenouillère. Advertisements like this increased the popularity of both resorts and the railroads in the late nineteenth century.

FUN NAMES ♦
In French, *La Grenouillère* means "frog pool." The island dominated by a large tree was called "camembert" because it was shaped like a wheel of camembert cheese.

THE ISLAND ♦
People often gathered on the island in front of the restaurant.

SWIMMING ♦
La Grenouillère offered swimming lessons. The classes for children took place in a separate, roped-off area.

FASHION ♦
Clothing at the resort ranged from bathing suits to stylish dresses and suits.

The Artists
Monet and Renoir often worked side-by-side as they painted at La Grenouillère. Some consider the paintings they produced there to be the first Impressionist masterpieces. Both have elements that became characteristic of the Impressionist style: an outdoor scene of people at leisure, vivid colors, quick brushstrokes suggesting foliage and figures, and sunlight reflecting on water. In Monet's painting, the bright sunshine in the background contrasts with the cool shadows in the foreground. The light "feels" real, not like the artificial light of paintings done in a studio. Both paintings also have an informality not found in academic painting. Objects are cropped off at the edge of the frame, and both artists chose to portray the overall atmosphere of the place, instead of focusing attention on one dominant feature.

♦ BAZILLE'S BATHERS
Bathing, or swimming, in the Seine was a popular pastime during the summer and a frequent subject of Impressionist paintings. This work from 1869 was done by Frédéric Bazille, a friend of Monet's.

✦ SAILBOATS
Boat races were a popular attraction at La Grenouillère. Bazille, Monet, and Renoir participated in some of the races.

✦ BOAT RENTALS
Beneath the restaurant were wooden boats that could be hired for short trips on the Seine.

MONET'S ✦ COMPOSITION
Water is the main feature of Monet's painting of La Grenouillère. Monet was fascinated by light, especially its reflections on water.

✦ RENOIR'S STUDY
In Renoir's painting, the wooden boats, the tree on the island, and the visitors in fashionable clothing are the focal points.

CAFÉ LIFE

When they weren't busy painting, the Impressionists could often be found at the Café Guerbois (gehr bwah). The café was located in the Batignolles (bah teen yohl) district of Paris. Many of the artists lived in the neighborhood. Cafés were at the center of Parisian social life. Much more than just places to get a meal, they offered a place for people to relax and enjoy each other's company. There were many kinds of cafés, including those frequented by intellectuals, those frequented by bankers and politicians, and those for the working class. The Guerbois was popular with artists and writers. It was a noisy place, full of heated discussions about art and literature.

✦ SIDEWALK CAFÉS
Cafés extended out onto the sidewalks of the broad, new boulevards. The large café awnings became a familiar feature of Paris.

✦ RENOIR
Despite his talent as an artist, Renoir struggled financially during the years he frequented the Guerbois. The Salon regularly rejected the paintings he submitted for exhibition.

✦ DEGAS
Degas had met Manet while copying paintings at the Louvre. He was a frequent visitor to the Guerbois.

✦ MANET
Manet was bold, witty, and self-confident. He was often the focus of attention in the group and tended to dominate the discussions.

✦ BAZILLE
Bazille was from a wealthy family and came to Paris in the 1860s to study medicine, but soon abandoned those plans to pursue a career as an artist.

✦ ZOLA
Émile Zola was a popular French writer closely aligned to the Realist movement. He was a staunch supporter of Manet and wrote articles in his defense when the art critics turned against him.

♦ HIGH SOCIETY
Cafés were not just for artists or the working class. There were elegant, high-society cafés for wealthy Parisians.

♦ THE CAFÉ
In a sketch from 1869, inspired by the Café Guerbois, Manet captured the atmosphere of an artists' meeting place. The people gathered around the marble-topped table are engaged in lively conversation.

♦ MONET
Monet formed close friendships with the other Impressionists. During the 1860s, he was often traveling, but when he returned to Paris, he enjoyed conversing with his fellow artists at the Guerbois.

♦ PISSARRO
Pissarro was the oldest member of the group. Although he lived outside of Paris, he visited the Guerbois when he came to town. He enjoyed socializing and sharing ideas with the other artists.

♦ THE STUDIO
In 1870, Henri Fantin-Latour, a friend of Manet and a frequent visitor to the Guerbois, portrayed a studio in the Batignolles district. Manet is in the middle of a group of artists that includes Renoir, Monet, and Bazille, and Astruc.

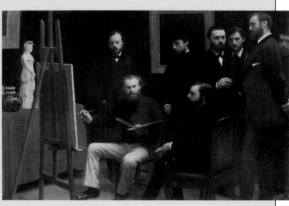

♦ CÉZANNE
Émile Zola was a childhood friend of Cézanne's and convinced the artist to move to Paris. Though he lived in Paris for only a short time, Cézanne became acquainted with the Impressionists and sometimes joined them at the Guerbois.

♦ ASTRUC
Zacharie Astruc was a poet, sculptor, and art critic. He was an enthusiastic supporter of the Impressionists.

THE ARTISTS
The artists who met regularly at the Café Guerbois included Édouard Manet, Pierre-Auguste Renoir, Frédéric Bazille, Edgar Degas, and Claude Monet. Paul Cézanne and Camille Pissarro sometimes joined them. Manet discovered the café in the late 1860s. At the time, many of the artists were struggling to get their work recognized. They found support among each other and also in Émile Zola, a French writer and member of the group who defended their work in the face of often hostile criticism. The café provided a place where the artists could discuss their work, share ideas, and plan their exhibitions.

LEISURE TIME

The Industrial Revolution changed the face of Paris and brought prosperity to the city. Out of that prosperity emerged a middle class that could afford to spend money on leisure. Paris offered plenty of opportunities for recreation. During the day, there was strolling in the parks, swimming, boating, and horse racing. At night, there were restaurants, theaters, and cafés. The Impressionists used their quick brushstrokes and colorful palettes to capture the festive atmosphere at all of these venues. Renoir depicted the carefree crowds at outdoor restaurants and dance halls. Degas, who was fascinated by movement, caught race horses in mid-stride and ballerinas in rehearsal. Cassatt's paintings of fashionable people at the opera illustrate another favorite pastime: Parisians watching themselves!

✦ **THE MOULIN ROUGE**
In this lithograph, or print, from 1891, Henri de Toulouse-Lautrec depicts the Moulin Rouge, a famous Paris nightclub, and its main attraction, "La Goulue," a dancer who performed there.

THE CAFÈ ✦ AND RESTAURANT
With the rise of the middle class, cafés and restaurants played a key role in the social life of Paris. Prior to that time, one ate at a restaurant out of necessity; now it was entertainment. Eating places ranged from elegant restaurants to casual, outdoor cafés.

1. Renoir, *The Boating Party*
2. Manet, *Chez Père Lathuille*
3. Degas, *Woman on a Café Terrace*
4. Manet, *A Bar at the Folies-Bergère*
5. Renoir, *At the Inn of Mother Anthony*

THE RACETRACK ✦
On weekends and public holidays, Parisians enjoyed watching horse racing. The racetrack was a popular place to meet and be seen, and the races themselves were exciting. Many Impressionist painters, Manet and Degas in particular, liked to paint racing scenes.

1. Degas, *Racehorses in front of the Stands*
2. Manet, *Horse Racing at Longchamps*
3. Degas, *The Gentlemen's Race*
4. Degas, *At the Races*

The theater became a frequent subject of Impressionist paintings. Degas portrayed the movements of ballerinas, and Manet and Cassatt depicted wealthy people at the opera. The artists were attracted by all aspects of the theater: the backstage rehearsal, the performance on stage, and the reaction of people in the audience.

1. Manet, *Masked Ball at the Opera*
2. Degas, *Café-concert*
3. Degas, *The Star*

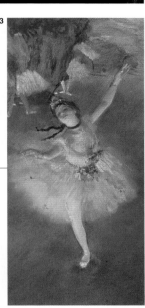

DANCING ✦

Dancing became very popular during the nineteenth century and dance halls opened up all over Paris. Renoir captured the colorful crowds and joyful atmosphere in many of his paintings.

1. Renoir, *Dance at the Moulin de la Galette*
2. Renoir, *A Dance in the Country*
3. Renoir, *A Dance in the City*

WAR COMES TO PARIS

The Franco-Prussian War began in July 1870, and by September, Paris was under siege. The Prussians blockaded the city until January 1871, when France surrendered. Despite the hardships they had suffered during the blockade, many citizens of Paris were outraged by the surrender. Fueled by resentment over the war and the new French government in Versailles, they revolted in March 1871 and established a revolutionary republic called The Paris Commune. The city was plunged into civil war. For the next two months, the army of the government in Versailles battled armed citizens in the streets of Paris. The Commune was ultimately defeated in late May 1871.

♦ NADAR'S HOT-AIR BALLOON
During the Prussian blockade of Paris, photographer Félix Nadar demonstrated that hot-air balloons could be used to get mail in and out of Paris and to send military messages across enemy lines.

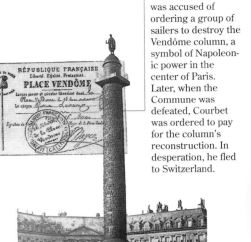

♦ THE COLUMN
Gustave Courbet was accused of ordering a group of sailors to destroy the Vendôme column, a symbol of Napoleonic power in the center of Paris. Later, when the Commune was defeated, Courbet was ordered to pay for the column's reconstruction. In desperation, he fled to Switzerland.

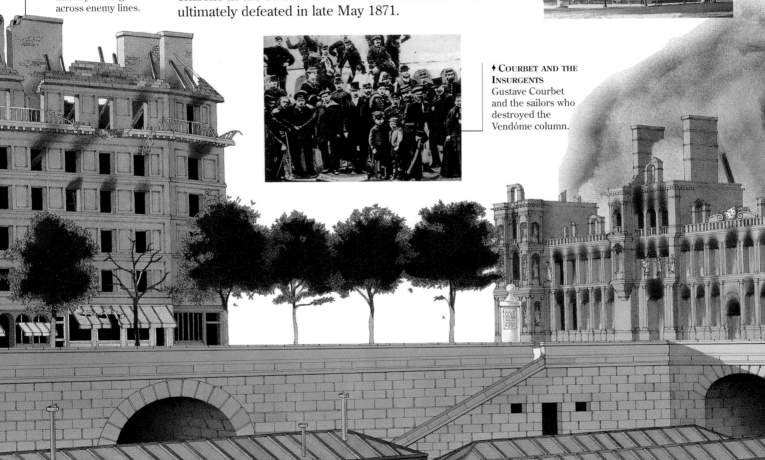

♦ COURBET AND THE INSURGENTS
Gustave Courbet and the sailors who destroyed the Vendôme column.

♦ BAZILLE'S DEATH
The only one of the Impressionists to fight on the front lines, Frédéric Bazille, here in a portrait by Renoir, enrolled in the French light infantry. He was killed on November 28, 1870. He was only twenty-nine.

THE BARRICADES ♦
Manet was in Paris during the Prussian siege. *The Barricade*, right, is one of a series of lithographs he did depicting the devastation of the city during the war.

THE ARTISTS

War ended the carefree café life at the Guerbois. Most of the Impressionists had little time or desire for painting. Manet and Degas both served in the National Guard. Renoir joined the cavalry. Bazille enlisted in the army soon after war was declared and was killed in November 1870 at the age of twenty-nine. Some artists took refuge outside of Paris. Cézanne returned to southern France. Monet and Pissarro went to London. In Paris, Gustave Courbet, the master of Realism, became a supporter of the Paris Commune and was later arrested for his affiliation. The Impressionists gradually returned to Paris once peace was restored.

♦ DEATH AND DEVASTATION
Paris suffered greatly during the war and the civil war that followed. Thousands of people were killed and hundreds of houses and shops were burned. The violence continued even after the Commune's collapse as many of the Communards were sentenced to death.

THE FIRST EXHIBITION

♦ **A NEW JOURNAL**
After the first exhibition, Monet and his fellow painters founded a magazine called "L'Impressioniste" to counter the critics and build support for their future shows. There were eight Impressionist exhibitions altogether: in 1874, 1876, 1877, 1879, 1880, 1881, 1882, and 1886.

Even more than their painting style, what united the Impressionists as a group was their objection to the Salon and the Salon's objection to their work. After the first Salon des Réfuses in 1863, the artists petitioned for similar exhibitions in 1867 and 1872, but they were denied. In 1874, they banded together and organized their own independent exhibition. It was held in Félix Nadar's studio and opened on April 15 — two weeks before the official Salon. The artists wanted to make it clear that these were not rejected works. Among the artists who exhibited were Degas, Pissarro, Renoir, Monet, Sisley, Morisot, and Cézanne. A total of 163 works were shown. Although 3,500 people attended the show, the reaction of the public and critics was negative, and only a few paintings were sold, at low prices.

♦ **AN HISTORIC PLACE**
It was here in Félix Nadar's studio on the Boulevard des Capucines that the Impressionists held their first exhibition in 1874.

♦ **EXHIBITION CATALOG**
Edmond Renoir, the brother of Pierre-Auguste, produced the catalog, shown above, for the first Impressionist exhibition.

♦ **FIRST IMPRESSION**
Scorned by the critics, this painting by Monet, titled *Impression: Sunrise*, was the work that gave rise to the term "Impressionism."

♦ **SATIRE**
In a satirical cartoon, Impressionist paintings are used to frighten away enemy soldiers.

CÉZANNE ✦
He showed three works at the 1874 exhibition. *The House of the Hanged Man,* painted in 1873–1874, is one of his most famous early works.

PISSARRO ✦
He exhibited five paintings, including *Hoarfrost,* an image of a winter sunrise in the country, painted in 1873.

DEGAS ✦
He exhibted ten works, including *Carriage at the Races,* painted between 1870–1872. Horse racing was a frequent subject of Degas's paintings.

MONET ✦
Of the twelve works exhibited by Monet, *Boulevard des Capucines, Paris,* painted in 1873, was one of the most shocking because of the sketchy way in which the pedestrians were painted.

THE ARTISTS

At the time of the 1874 exhibition, the artists referred to themselves as the "Anonymous society of painters, sculptors and engravers." They did not use the name "Impressionists." It was Louis Leroy, a French journalist and art critic, who coined the term. After seeing Monet's painting *Impression: Sunrise,* he ridiculed it, declaring that it was no more than an impression, and adding, "A preliminary drawing for a wallpaper pattern is more finished than this seascape!" Though some people were beginning to accept the Impressionists' style, most critics shared Leroy's opinion. To them, their bright colors were vulgar and their brushstrokes were sloppy compared to the smooth canvases of the academic painters. One critic, viewing a painting by Berthe Morisot, asked, "Why, with her talent, does she not take the trouble to finish?" Despite the criticism, the artists mounted seven more exhibitions over the next twelve years, and they gradually adopted the name Impressionists for themselves.

MORISOT ✦
Berthe Morisot, the only female among the Impressionists who participated in the 1874 exhibition, displayed nine works, including *The Cradle,* painted in 1873. Domestic scenes were frequent subjects of female painters at the time. It was considered improper for a woman to paint in public, especially outside on a city street.

RENOIR ✦
He exhibited seven works. *The Box at the Opera,* painted in 1874, is one of the first Impressionist works dedicated to the theater. Renoir took an active part in setting up the exhibition. He had the difficult task of deciding how best to display works that depicted a wide range of subjects.

THE CITY

Paris, as rebuilt by Haussmann, was the most modern city in Europe. Its new bridges and railroad stations were marvels of technology. Its broad new boulevards and grand public spaces were always filled with people. The Impressionists were stimulated by all of the activity and captured it on canvas. They were the first artists to treat a modern city as a subject in itself. They painted the crowds on the avenues and stylish Parisians strolling through the parks. The rows of new apartment buildings with their tall, graceful facades, provided an elegant backdrop to their scenes of urban life. The Impressionists also used the city to explore their ongoing fascination with light. Like their landscapes, they painted the city at different times of the day and in all kinds of weather.

♦ PARISIAN APARTMENTS
This illustration shows the interior of a typical apartment building constructed during Haussmann's redevelopment of Paris. The wealthiest people lived on the lower floors, where the rooms were large and had high ceilings. The middle classes lived above them. At the very top were servants, students, and artists. They had the smallest rooms, the lowest ceilings, and the longest climb up the stairs.

PANORAMAS ♦
The new Paris was full of large public spaces. To give a sense of their scale, the Impressionists often painted them from a high vantage point. Bridges were another favorite subject. They, too, were often painted from above in order to capture all the traffic crossing the Seine.

1. Monet, *Jardin de l'Infante*
2. Pissarro, *Boieldieu Bridge, Rouen*
3. Renoir, *Pont Neuf*

CROWDS ♦
Haussmann's wide boulevards were crowded with people and bustling with activity. The Impressionists portrayed the atmosphere of the boulevards at all times of the day and throughout the year.

1. Monet, *Boulevard des Capucines*
2. Monet, *Rue Montorgueil Decked Out with Flags*
3. Pissarro, *Boulevard Montmartre, Night Effect*

STROLLING IN ♦ THE CITY
Impressionist paintings often depicted Parisians promenading through the parks or strolling on the city's busy streets.

1. Monet, *Quai du Louvre*
2. Caillebotte, *Paris, A Rainy Day*
3. Renoir, *Place Clichy*

THE ART MARKET

For most of the nineteenth century, the Salon controlled the art market in France. It fixed prices and dictated which art was worth buying. Artists the Salon disapproved of had difficulty selling their work. The market began to change, however, with the emergence of the art dealer. While the Salon sold mainly to museums and other large institutions, art dealers bought work and resold it on the private market. Many of them took risks promoting young artists who were not yet established. Paul Durand-Ruel was a visionary art dealer who played a key role in the Impressionists' eventual success. The first to recognize the value of their work, he was their most vigorous promoter and was responsible for bringing Impressionism to the English and American markets.

MANET ✦
Caillebotte often helped support his fellow artists by buying their work. He purchased Manet's *The Balcony* in 1884.

MONET ✦
Monet painted huge canvases in the 1860s, including this portrait of his wife, *Camille (The Green Dress)*. He turned to smaller paintings when he had difficulty selling the large works.

RENOIR ✦
Pont Neuf, 1872. One of twenty paintings Renoir sold at the Hôtel Drouot auction in March 1875.

MONET ✦
Blue House in Zandaam, bought by Ernest Hoschedé, a wealthy client of Durand-Ruel and early collector of Monet, sold at auction for a low price in 1878 when Hoschedé declared bankruptcy.

SISLEY ✦
Floods at Port-Marly, 1876, sold at auction in 1878 for the low sum of 180 French francs. After Sisley's death in 1900, the painting was sold for 43,000 francs, more than Sisley had earned in his entire lifetime.

✦ THE AUCTION ROOM
Public auctions were one way for artists to sell their work. Auctions in Paris were held at the Hôtel Drouot, which hosted the sale of Impressionist paintings in 1875.

♦ **PAUL DURAND-RUEL**
1831–1922
He was the first art dealer to invest in the Impressionists.

♦ **VICTOR CHOCQUET**
1821–1891
He admired the art of past masters, but also bought Impressionist paintings, especially Cézanne.

♦ **GEORGES PETIT**
1856–1920
Petit was a shrewd businessman and a rival of Durand-Ruel. He organized exhibits of Impressionist art in his gallery, which can be seen in this print.

THE ARTISTS

The Impressionists' first exhibit in 1874 was a failure from both a critical and financial standpoint. A year later, many of the artists were still struggling financially. They decided to hold an auction of their unsold paintings at the Hôtel Drouot in March 1875. The Hôtel Druuot, opened in 1852, was the largest auction house in Paris. The paintings that sold at the auction fetched low prices and the art critics who attended were still hostile to the Impressionists' work. Fortunately, there were influential art dealers like Durand-Ruel who continued to champion the artists. In 1876, Durand-Ruel hosted their second exhibition in his Paris gallery and continued to promote their work with exhibitions in his London gallery.

♦ **CÉZANNE**
The House of the Hanged Man failed to sell at the 1875 auction but was purchased in 1899 for 6,200 francs, a sign of Cézanne's growing fame.

♦ **RENOIR**
Bids were low at the auction of unsold works at the Hôtel Drouot in 1875. Renoir's *Pont des Arts, Paris*, 1867, sold for only 70 francs (less than $50).

The portal, morning fog

The portal, morning effect

The portal, harmony in blue

The portal, harmony in brown

LIGHT

For an Impressionist, light was often the true subject of a canvas, and a street scene or landscape simply a pretext for exploring its changing qualities. In the 1890s, Monet conducted some of the most in-depth studies of light by painting the same subject under a variety of light conditions. One of the most famous of these studies is his Rouen Cathedral series, painted between 1892 and 1894. Monet produced over thirty views of the cathedral, portraying it in all types of light: at dawn and sunset, in sunshine and

Harmony in blue and gold, bright sun

The portal, sunshine

Rouen Cathedral, sun effect, late in the day

Symphony in gray and pink

The portal, harmony in gray, dull weather *Rouen Cathedral, the portal*   *Rouen Cathedral, the portal*   *The portal, midday*

rain, in summer and winter. Monet's goal was not to paint pictures of a cathedral. In fact, most of the building is cropped out of the frame. His intent was to use the cathedral's facade, with its intricate carving and recessed windows and arches, to record changes in light and atmosphere. The Rouen series is one of the masterpieces of Impressionist painting. It was also a novel idea. Producing thirty canvases on the same subject was unusual in painting. It also proved to be successful for Monet. Durand-Ruel displayed twenty of the paintings in his gallery in 1895 and sold them rapidly. Even art critics praised the series.

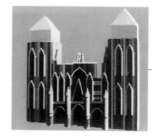

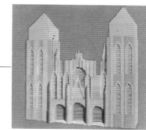

♦ THE SEASONS
The four images on the left are computer simulations of light conditions at Rouen Cathedral — in different seasons and at different times of day — as Monet would have experienced them. Clockwise, from top left, the light conditions at 2:00 P.M. on December 23; at 2:00 P.M. on March 21; and at 2:00 P.M. and 7:00 P.M. on June 21.

The Portal and Alban Tower, dull weather *Harmony in white*   *The portal, sunshine*   *The Portal and Alban Tower, dawn*

THEIR LEGACY

Impressionism represents a major turning point in Western art. For centuries, the art world had been dominated by the traditional views endorsed by the art academies and institutions like the Salon. The Impressionists defied tradition and followed their own instincts, even in the face of persistent ridicule and rejection. As the images on these pages illustrate, Impressionism is at the root of modern art. It broke the rules regarding color and composition. It introduced new painting techniques in its use of short, conspicuous brushstrokes. Inspired by photography, it experimented with cropping, perspective, and the blurring of figures. Instead of glorifying the past, the Impressionists celebrated everyday modern life. In their refusal to allow the Salon to dictate how and what to paint, the Impressionists paved the way for the groundbreaking artists of the twentieth century.

✦ **EUGÈNE DELACROIX**
1798–1863

✦ **PABLO PICASSO**
1881–1973

The Artists

In 1886, Durand-Ruel organized a major exhibition of Impressionist paintings in New York. It was such a success that he soon opened a New York gallery. He and other art dealers continued to promote the Impressionists in Europe and some of their works were acquired by museums. These sales brought long-awaited financial stability to some of the artists. Monet was able to buy his home in Giverny, where he painted well into his eighties. Renoir also prospered, and lived long enough to see one of his paintings enter the Louvre. 1886 also witnessed the Impressionists' eighth and final exhbition together. By that time, the group had begun to disband. Cézanne had retreated to Provence, where he was developing his own style. Pissarro dabbled in Pointillism, and Degas, nearly blind, had turned to sculpture.

✦ **DELACROIX**
Liberty Leading the People, 1830, Eugène Delacroix (1798–1863). Delacroix's emotionally charged painting of the French Revolution epitomizes Romanticism, an art movement of the early nineteenth century. Romantic paintings emphasized emotion and heroism and often depicted historic events.

✦ **MONET**
Monet's light-filled painting, *The Artist's House at Argenteuil,* 1873, shows the evolution of painting styles that followed Romanticism: ordinary life as subject matter; short, visible brushstrokes creating the illusion of leaves, flowers, and figures; and a canvas filled with light.

✦ **SEURAT**
Sunday Afternoon on the Island of La Grande Jatte, (1886) by Georges Seurat (1851–1891) is an example of Neo-Impressionism, also known as Pointillism. Painters in this style shared the Impressionists' bright palettes and subject matter, but created works entirely out of small dots of color, instead of using brushstrokes.

✦ **MATISSE**
Luxe, Calme et Volupté (1904–1905). During the first years of the twentieth century, Henri Matisse (1869–1959) was a leading figure in a movement called Fauvism. The Fauves took Impressionism to the extreme by eliminating everything that was not color from the canvas.

♦ INGRES AND CABANEL

Jean Auguste Dominique Ingres (1780–1867) was a rival of Delacroix. He believed drawing was more important than color in a painting. Left: His *Le Bain Turc (Turkish Bath)*, 1862, influenced Degas. Right: *The Birth of Venus*, 1863, by Alexandre Cabanel (1823–1889). Cabanel was a traditional academic painter.

GAUGUIN

Paul Gauguin (1848–1903) exhibited with the Impressionists and assimilated their techniques before developing his own distinctive style. He eventually left Europe for the islands of Polynesia. *The Beach at Dieppe*, 1885, is an example of his early, Impressionist work.

♦ TOULOUSE-LAUTREC

Henri de Toulouse-Lautrec was famous for his prints and paintings of Parisian nightlife. Degas was a major influence on his work. Left: Toulouse-Lautrec (1864–1901) *At the Moulin Rouge*, 1892. One of his most popular paintings, this work used unusual perspective, bold colors, and a graphic style.

♦ VAN GOGH AND MUNCH

Left: Vincent Van Gogh (1853–1890), *Wheatfield with Crows*, 1890. Van Gogh was influenced by Impressionism and inspired the movement known as Expresssionism. Edvard Munch (1863–1944), an Expressionist, was initially influenced by Pissarro and Monet, as can be seen in his *Rue Lafayette*, 1891 (right).

CÉZANNE

The paintings of Paul Cézanne (1839–1906) form a bridge between the nineteenth and twentieth centuries. In his *House on a Hill* (1904–1906), right, he constructed his subject with geometric precision. His style inspired Cubism, one of the most important art movements of the twentieth century.

♦ PICASSO

Cubism began with *Les demoiselles d'Avignon* (left) painted in 1907 by Pablo Picasso (1881–1973). Cézanne was the link between Impressionism and Cubism. Here, his influence on Picasso is obvious in the abstract bodies and geometric shapes.

ÉDOUARD MANET

Although Édouard Manet is associated with Impressionism, his painting style represents a link between Realism and Impressionism. His palette was dark, like the Realists, and he placed great emphasis on drawing, whereas Impressionist figures were looser and less finished. Manet was revered by the Impressionists and he socialized with them, but he never exhibited with the group. He preferred the prestige of the Salon, even though it repeatedly rejected his work. Encouraged by his friend Berthe Morisot, Manet experimented with painting *en plein air,* but he never gave up painting in the studio.

♦ WITH FRIENDS
Manet (right) with Méry Laurent, an actress and artists' model, and the poet Stéphane Mallarmé, photographed in 1872.

HIS LIFE
Édouard Manet was born in Paris in 1832, to a well-to-do family. His parents wanted him to study law, but he wanted to become an aritst. At age eighteen, he began studying at the studio of Thomas Couture. He also went to the Louvre Museum to study the works of Italian and Spanish masters. Manet is often considered one of the Impressionists, yet he did not take part in any of

their exhibitions. He preferred to exhibit at the Salon. He met with some success there, but many of his paintings were rejected. *Luncheon on the Grass*, painted in 1863, was the first of his "scandalous" works. It was followed in 1865 by *Olympia*, which met with even more scorn. Manet did not find the success and recognition he sought until rather late in his career. In 1881, he was awarded the Legion of Honor, France's highest honor for civilians. He died in 1883.

Luncheon on the Grass
Manet's most famous painting, *Luncheon on the Grass*, caused a scandal. Its composition respects all the traditional rules. In fact, its inspiration was a sixteenth-century work. What upset people was seeing a nude woman in a modern setting; especially a nude woman lunching with two men. Nudes in art were acceptable only as mythical figures. The painting's large size—81.9 x 104.5 inches (208 by 265 cm)—added to its shock value. The critics' disdain for the work only increased Manet's stature among his fellow artists.

♦ AN INSPIRATION
The Judgment of Paris, by Marcantonio Raimondi, c. 1515, was the work that inspired *Luncheon on the Grass*.

♦ LANDSCAPES
The trees in the background are painted in a style reminiscent of the Barbizon school, a group of French landscape painters who were the first to use the technique of painting *en plein air*.

♦ THE SUBJECT
The portrayal of a naked woman with two men dressed in modern clothing, recognized as Manet's brother and future brother-in-law, shocked the public. A nude figure was tolerated only in historical or mythological scenes.

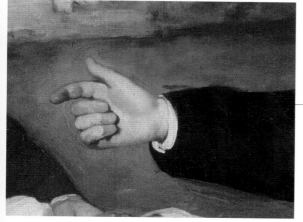

♦ AN ISOLATED POSE
The gesture of the man on the right implies that the two men are engaged in conversation. The figures in the painting are lit theatrically.

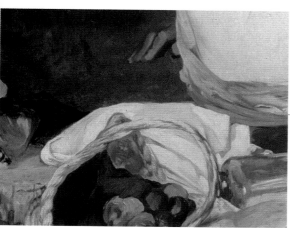

♦ STILL LIFE
Manet painted the basket of fruit in the left foreground in the style of a still life, bringing a traditional element into the painting.

♦ A SCANDALOUS SUBJECT
In *The Absinthe Drinker*, painted in 1859, Manet depicted an alcoholic. The Salon jury rejected the work.

♦ AT THE TUILERIES
In 1862, Manet painted *Music in the Tuileries Gardens*, which depicts a crowd of fashionable people attending an open-air concert in a Paris park.

THE CORRIDA ♦
Painted in 1862, *M.lle Victorine in the costume of an Espada* reflects Manet's interest in bullfighting.

AMERICAN WAR ♦
An espisode from the American Civil War, *The Battle of the Kearsage and the Alabama* (fought off the coast of France) was painted in 1864.

CLAUDE MONET

It is fitting that a painting by Monet inspired the name "impressionism." His dedication to working *en plein air* and his canvases filled with light and color personify the movement. Monet worked quickly, applying paint with short, swift brush-strokes so he could record every detail he saw before his eyes. Monet studied his subjects carefully and noticed every color, every subtle change in atmosphere. Leaving behind the somber tones of earlier landscape painting, Monet saturated his canvases with color, whether he was depicting the sun-drenched countryside or a cold winter day.

✦ **WATERLILIES**
Monet painting one of his large canvases dedicated to waterlilies.

HIS LIFE

Born in Paris in 1840, Claude Monet grew up in the French coastal city of Le Havre, where he attended a local school for the arts. At the age of twenty, he moved to Paris to make a career as an artist. In Paris, he met the other Impressionists and studied painting in earnest — at the Louvre, the École des Beaux-Arts, and in the studios of private masters. During the 1860s, Monet concentrated on painting *en plein air* with Bazille, Renoir, and Sisley. When war broke out between France and Prussia in 1870, Monet took shelter in London. There, he met the art dealer Paul Durand-Ruel, who would become instrumental in boosting the careers of all the Impressionists. Monet returned to France in 1871, and took part in the group's first exhibition in 1874. He struggled financially for most of his career, but finally met with success in the 1880s and 1890s. In 1890, he bought his home in Giverny, north-west of Paris, where he continued to paint until his death in 1926.

HAYSTACKS, END OF SUMMER

In the summer of 1890, Monet began painting haystacks near his home outside of Paris. Haystacks were a common feature in the country-side. For Monet, their simple shapes became the basis for studying the effects of light. He was intrigued by the way the colors in the highlights and shadows changed throughout the day. In the end, Monet painted twenty-five views of the haystacks. He documented the scene at different times of day and throughout the fall and winter. In the painting above, the haystacks are aglow in the shimmering heat of a bright summer's day. When the series was complete, Monet exhibited fifteen of the haystack canvases at Durand-Ruel's gallery. Every painting sold within days.

✦ **OLD AGE**
Monet in his Giverny studio, photographed at the beginning of the twentieth century.

VÉTHEUIL IN ✦ SUMMER
In 1879, Monet spent a few months in this small town on the Seine, north of Paris. He painted several views of it.

IN ITALY ✦
At the end of 1883, Monet took a trip to the Italian riviera. *Lemon Trees at Bordighera* is one of his works from that period.

✦ LIGHTING
To achieve the effect of sunlight on the larger of the two haystacks, Monet used warm colors ranging from red through orange to pink, with touches of bright white. The shadows and the trees and hills in the background are composed of cool blues and greens. Monet's thick brushstrokes mirror the coarseness of the hay.

✦ LILY POND
The waterlilies in his pond at Giverny provided Monet with an unending source of inspiration.

✦ BOAT RACES
Monet lived in Argenteuil from 1872–1876. *Regatta at Argenteuil*, 1872, is an example of his fascination with reflections on water.

VÉTHEUIL ✦ IN WINTER
In this winter scene, Monet used pale tones for the snow and dark, cool colors to depict the Seine, which was nearly frozen.

PIERRE-AUGUSTE RENOIR

Renoir once proclaimed, "For me a picture should be a pleasant thing, joyful and pretty — yes, pretty!" This statement explains the popularity of Renoir's most well-known works, which are full of luminous color and youthful Parisians at leisure. His scenes of outdoor restaurants and light-filled gardens reflect the carefree spirit that infected Paris at the end of the nineteenth century. Renoir often painted with Monet, but Monet tended to focus on nature, while Renoir was more interested in people. He painted portraits throughout his career and his figures are full of expression.

♦ THE BATHERS
The painting above was Renoir's last work, completed in 1919. He had depicted bathers in the 1880s (below). At that time, Renoir's style had changed and he used the clear outlines and formal composition he had seen on a trip to Italy to study the old masters. In the 1890s, he returned to his earlier style, which was all soft brushwork and light.

HIS LIFE
The son of a tailor, Pierre-Auguste Renoir was born in 1841 in Limoges. His talent for drawing was already apparent as an adolescent and he got a job in a porcelain factory painting designs on plates. In Paris, he copied masters at the Louvre and studied in the studio of Charles Gleyre, where he met Monet, Sisley, and Bazille. He and Monet often painted together. Renoir took part in many of the Impressionist exhibitions. He struggled financially during the 1860s, but met with success in the 1870s, thanks to Durand-Ruel's gallery and commissions from several wealthy patrons. In the 1880s, Renoir traveled to Algeria, Spain, and Italy, and his painting style briefly changed. He suffered from severe arthritis during the last twenty years of his life, but continued to work. In the end, he had to strap a brush to his hand in order to paint. He died in 1919.

DANCE AT THE MOULIN DE LA GALETTE
The Moulin de la Galette was a popular dance hall in the Montmartre district of Paris. It attracted large crowds, especially on weekend afternoons. Renoir captured the lively atmosphere on canvas in 1876. He was known for his feathery brushstrokes, which give his paintings a soft look. Here, the softness adds to the sense of movement, blurring the dancing figures. The outdoor setting is conveyed by the sun-dappled effect on the dance floor and the young man seated in the foreground.

◆ IN ARGENTEUIL
Sailboats at Argenteuil, painted in 1874, shows Monet's influence. Monet was inspired by the same subject.

◆ PART OF A LARGER SCENE
Placing figures at the edges of the painting gives the impression that the scene carries on beyond the canvas.

◆ CONTRASTS
The white lights and pale dresses of the women contrast sharply with the dark clothing of the men.

◆ THE GARDEN
During the time he was painting *Dance at the Moulin de la Galette*, Renoir was living in a rented studio on the Rue Cortot in the Montmartre district. What appealed to Renoir most about his new studio was the garden outside. It was wild and overgrown, but full of color. His delight in the garden is evident in his painting *The Garden of the Rue Cortot*. Each day, his friends helped him carry the large canvas of *Dance at the Moulin de la Galette* into the garden, where Renoir concentrated on putting the finishing touches to the painting.

◆ ARAB FESTIVAL
Renoir traveled widely in the 1880s. In 1881, he visited Algeria, where he painted this scene of people at a festival. The heat of the day is reflected in their white clothing, the white buildings in the background, and the golden hillside.

EDGAR DEGAS

Edgar Degas studied at the conservative École des Beaux-Arts and began his career painting traditional subjects. Later, he was drawn to contemporary themes, but unlike his fellow Impressionists, he preferred painting in the studio. "What I do is the result of thought and study . . . ," he remarked. "I know nothing about inspiration, spontaneity, and feeling." Degas was not interested in nature or painting *en plein air*. Because of his academic training, he held drawing in great respect. This served him well in his many depictions of dancers. In the 1870s, Degas's vision began deteriorating and he gradually turned to sculpture.

♦ IN THE OMNIBUS
Degas shows a couple on a horse-drawn bus, an early form of mass transit. Degas himself enjoyed people-watching on the omnibus.

HIS LIFE
Born in Paris in 1843, Degas was the son of a French banker. His mother was an American from New Orleans. Degas set out to study law, but decided instead to become an artist. He studied at the prestigious École des Beaux-Arts, where he perfected his drawing skills. He also traveled extensively to study the works of the old masters. He began his artistic career painting religious and historical subjects and portraits of wealthy families. This gave him financial stability. After meeting Manet in 1862, he became interested in painting contemporary life and joined the regular meetings of the Impressionists at the Café Guerbois. Degas served in the National Guard during the Franco-Prussian War. In 1872, he spent five months with his American relatives in New Orleans. After returning to Paris, he took part in almost all of the Impressionists' group exhibitions. Degas experimented with various techniques, including pastels. When his eyes began to fail him, he turned to sculpture. In the last years of his life, Degas was nearly blind. He became increasingly reclusive and died alone in Paris in September 1917.

THE REHEARSAL OF THE BALLET ONSTAGE
Dancers were a common theme for Degas, even in his sculptures. He was more interested in what went on behind the scenes than the actual performance. This painting of a rehearsal reveals Degas's fondness for asymmetrical compositions and odd cropping: the dancer on the left edge of the painting is virtually cut in half. Degas enjoyed working with pastels and this painting is a combination of pastels and oils. He preferred the artificial light of the theater to natural light. He once said, "The fascinating thing is not to show the source of light, but the effect of light."

♦ SCULPTURE
Preliminary study for *Little Fourteen-Year-Old Dancer* (left), and the finished sculpture (right). Degas and Renoir were the only Impressionists to take up sculpture.

♦ BALLERINAS
Degas showed his talent for drawing in the way he sketched ballerinas. Before beginning the painting, he made a series of preparatory drawings, studying the dancers' positions and movements and the contours of their limbs.

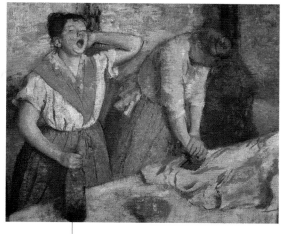
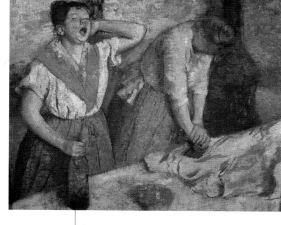

♦ IN THE BACKGROUND
The two men in the background appear to be bored with the endless hours of rehearsal. Degas enjoyed capturing the backstage scenes that the audience never saw.

♦ WOMEN IRONING
Despite his aristocratic upbringing, Degas was interested in the lives of ordinary working people and often depicted them in his paintings. *Women Ironing*, painted in 1884–1886, is one example.

♦ NUDES
Getting out of the Bath. In academic painting, nudes were usually mythical subjects. Degas's nudes were ordinary people taking a bath or getting dressed in the morning.

♦ WEARINESS
Degas depicted the weariness of long rehearsals. Here, a young dancer on the sidelines yawns and stretches during a moment of rest.

♦ ABSINTHE
Absinthe was a popular drink among writers and artists in the late nineteenth century. It had a very high alcohol content and was believed to be addictive. Here, Degas has shown the darker side of café life by portraying two people in an alcoholic stupor brought on by drinking absinthe.

♦ THE MASTER
Degas used the figure of the ballet master, painted in dark colors, to separate the two main sections of the painting: the ballerinas rehearsing on the right, and those waiting their turn on the left.

PAUL CÉZANNE

Paul Cézanne was introduced to Impressionist tehniques through his friendship with Camille Pissarro, whom he met soon after arriving in Paris. Under Pissarro's influence, Cézanne began painting outdoors and adopted the bright palette and distinctive brushstrokes characteristic of Impressionism. Eventually, however, Cézanne sought something more "durable" than Impressionism. Returning to his native Provence, he created his own style, marked by simple, geometric forms and vivid blocks of color.

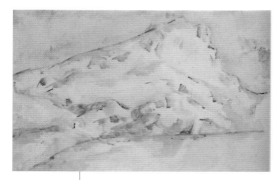

♦ A FAVORITE SUBJECT
Above and below: two more views of Mont Sainte-Victoire in Provence. Cézanne produced over fifty views of the mountain, painting it from different angles.

HIS LIFE
The son of a banker, Paul Cézanne was born in Provence, a region in southern France, in 1839. Cézanne began drawing at an early age, but studied law to please his father. In 1861, he moved to Paris, against his family's wishes, to pursue an artistic career. His father eventually supported his decision and left Cézanne an inheritance that freed him from the financial worries suffered by many other painters. In Paris, he met Pissarro, who became a friend and mentor. The two painted many landscapes together, with Cézanne's palette becoming much lighter under Pissarro's influence. Cézanne's works were regularly rejected by the Salon. He exhibited with the Impressionists in 1874 and 1877, but moved back to Provence permanently in the early 1880s. Always shy, Cézanne became increasingly reclusive, working on his paintings in isolation. In 1895, Ambroise Vollard, an art dealer in Paris, held an exhibition of Cézanne's work. It was a great success and brought Cézanne to the attention of many younger artists. Near the end of his life, Cézanne suffered from diabetes. He died in Provence in 1906.

MONT SAINTE-VICTOIRE
The Sainte-Victoire mountain in Provence was visible from the home of Cézanne's brother-in-law. The peak became one of Cézanne's favorite subjects and he painted over fifty views of it between 1880–1883. To paint this view, Cézanne worked in an abandoned quarry. His use of geometric forms was ideal for depicting the rugged terrain: rectangular blocks of color for the hard quarry rocks; diagonal brushstrokes for the scraggy foliage; and a triangle for Mont Sainte-Victoire itself.

♦ THE SUMMIT
The bulk of the mountain, which seems to rise straight out of the quarry, was achieved with vertical gray strokes. The gray color not only adds depth to the painting, but simulates the actual color of the limestone peak.

♦ ROCKS
Cézanne used short, rectangular brush-strokes to create the rocks in the quarry. The shape of his brushwork reinforces the verticality of the cliffs, and the warm, golden colors reflect the sun's heat on the rocks.

THE CARDPLAYERS ♦
Cézanne produced a series of paintings of men playing cards. Here, the figures have the same solid quality as the table.

♦ TREES
Cézanne used diagonal brushstrokes to create the trees. The strokes are soft and blurred, emphasizing the suppleness of the trees compared to the firmness of the rocks.

♦ BATHERS
The Large Bathers, painted between 1898 and 1905, was one of Cézanne's final works. It is also his largest: 82-7/8 x 98 3/4 inches (210.5 x 250.8 cm), and the one he worked on the longest. The figures are almost abstract and the overall composition is that of a triangle.

♦ APPLES AND PEACHES
Cézanne was a master still-life painter. Fruit figures prominently in all of his still lifes. The appeal of fruit, such as the apples and peaches below, was the simplicity and perfection of its shape. Cézanne saw everything in terms of geometry and used fruit to practice depicting the spherical form.

CAMILLE PISSARRO

Camille Pissarro is often referred to as the father of the Impressionist movement. He was the most prolific of the group and the only one to participate in all eight of their independent exhibitions. Pissarro was also the eldest of the Impressionists. Younger painters turned to him for inspiration and advice. Pissarro enjoyed portraying landscapes as well as the busy boulevards of Paris. In his decidedly Impressionist works, he combined a lively sense of color with a balanced composition.

HIS LIFE

Born in Saint-Thomas, an island in the Caribbean, in 1830, Pissarro settled in Paris in 1855. He admired the work of the Barbizon school and was attracted to the idea of painting landscapes directly from nature. In Paris, he befriended the other Impressionists. Like them, he had been rejected by the Salon and eagerly participated in their independent exhibitions. During the Franco-Prussian War, he took refuge in London with Monet. There, he met the art dealer Paul Durand-Ruel. In 1893, Durand-Ruel held a major exhibition of Pissarro's works. Despite his support, Pissarro sold few paintings in his lifetime. In the late 1880s, he experimented with Pointillism, a painting style that used small dots of color instead of brushstrokes, but he returned to Impressionism in the last decade of his life. Pissarro died near Paris in November 1903.

♦ A FACTORY
In *Factory Near Pontoise,* Pissarro depicted a landscape that was both rural and industrial.

THE BACKWOODS AT L'HERMITAGE
Pissarro moved to Pointoise, a town near Paris, in 1872 and lived there for seventeen years. The town and its environs became the subject of many of his canvases. His painting of the Hermitage, a small village near Pontoise, is characteristic of an Impressionist landscape. Pissarro used short, rapid brushstrokes to create the leaves of the trees and a soft palette to give the effect of sunlight filtering through the foliage. The painting was finished in time for the Impressionists' fourth exhibition in 1879.

♦ PEASANTS
Young Woman Washing Dishes, 1882, marked a return of Pissarro's interest in peasants. The painting was one of thirty works Pissarro showed at the 1882 Impressionist exhibition.

ALFRED SISLEY

Alfred Sisley was above all a landscape painter. Unlike the other Impressionists, he was not interested in depicting urban scenes or painting portraits. He preferred painting the small country towns outside of Paris. Like Monet, Sisley was fascinated by the spectacle of changing light. Reflections on water and large, cloud-filled skies feature prominently in his work. His quiet, rural settings and sensitive use of color combine to create a feeling of tranquility.

♦ **FLOOD ON THE SEINE**
In 1876, the Seine overflowed its banks. Sisley depicted the scene in *Floods at Port-Marly.*

HIS LIFE
The son of a wealthy English merchant who settled in France, Sisley was born in Paris in 1839. He enrolled at the École des Beaux-Arts in 1861 and later attended the studio of Charles Gleyre, where he met Monet, Renoir, and Bazille. Sisley was part of the Café Guerbois group.

During the Franco-Prussian War, he took shelter in Louveciennes, a town west of Paris. He depicted the area in some of his paintings. In 1871, his father went bankrupt and soon died, leaving Sisley in disastrous financial straits. Monet and Pissarro introduced him to the art dealer Paul Durand-Ruel, who immediately bought some of his paintings. Sisley also took part in several Impressionist exhibitions, but his work met with criticism. It wasn't until after his death, in 1899, that his paintings achieved recognition and began selling for very high prices.

BOATS ON THE SEINE
Nature is the dominant factor in Sisley's paintings. Though people are present in *Boats on the Seine,* they are dwarfed by the enormous sky. Sisley emphasized the difference between the sky and the flat landscape below through his use of brushstrokes: horizontal for the river and the houses in the distance, and vertical and diagonal for the clouds above. The figures in the foreground are busy working, unlike the fashionable people at leisure normally seen in Impressionist paintings of the Seine.

♦ **LOUVECIENNES**
Rue de la Machine: The vast sky and the line of trees along the roadway create depth.

BERTHE MORISOT

Berthe Morisot became a successful artist at a time when women were not even allowed to enroll at the École des Beaux-Arts. Studying privately with master artists, she became an accomplished landscape painter whose works were regularly accepted by the Salon. In 1874, she was the only female artist to exhibit with the Impressionists at their first exhibition. In her lifetime, Morisot sold more paintings than her Impressionist colleagues.

✦ HARBOR OF LORIENT
Berthe Morisot's sister, Edma, often posed for her and was the model for this painting.

HER LIFE
Berthe Morisot was born in Bourges, a town in central France, in 1841. Her family supported her interest in art, but as a woman, she was not allowed to attend the École des Beaux-Arts. Instead, she studied privately in Paris with several masters, including Corot, a revered landscape painter, who introduced her to painting *en plein air.* Morisot exhibited regularly at the Salon until 1873. Then, influenced by her friendship with Manet, she began exhibiting with the Impressionists. She excelled at landscapes and domesic scenes. Both were deemed suitable subjects for female artists in the nineteenth century. She died in Paris in 1895.

✦ PORTRAIT BY MANET
Morisot and Manet shared a lifelong friendship, and each influenced the other's work. Manet became Morisot's brother-in-law in 1874, when she married his younger brother, Eugene.

✦ DOMESTIC SCENES
Morisot often depcited the private world of upper-class women like herself in her paintings. *Woman at Her Toilette*, painted in 1875, is an intimate scene of a woman styling her hair.

✦ QUAY AT BOUGIVAL
Painted in 1883, the setting is a town by the Seine, not far from Paris. The subtle tones of blue and cream unite the river, its banks, and the sky.

THE MOTHER AND SISTER OF THE ARTIST
Morisot's mother and sister, Edma, posed for this work, painted in 1869–1870. At the time, Edma was pregnant with her first child. She had studied painting with Berthe in Paris, but gave it up when she married. The painting was accepted by the Salon, but Morisot was still unsatisfied. She confessed her doubts to Manet, who made some changes without her permission. His hand is evident in the mother's face and black dress.

MARY CASSATT

Mary Cassatt is the only American painter associated with the Impressionists. Unlike her colleagues, however, Cassatt focused almost entirely on portraits. She is most well-known for her scenes of domestic life, particularly women and children. She admired Japanese art, and her drawings and etchings reveal the flat planes, patterned backgrounds, and simple lines typical of Japanese prints.

♦ THE CHILD'S BATH
Women and children feature prominently in Cassatt's work. This painting from 1893 features a high vantage point, close cropping, and patterns reminscent of Japanese prints.

HER LIFE
Mary Cassatt was born into a wealthy family in Pittsburgh, Pennsylvania, in 1845. Against her family's wishes, she pursued a career in art, studying first at the Pennsylvania Academy of Fine Arts, then moving to Paris in 1866, where she studied privately. In 1868, the prestigious Salon accepted one of her paintings. She returned to the United States during the Franco-Prussian War, but came back to Europe in 1871 and resumed painting. In 1874, she met Degas, who introduced her to the other Impressionists and encouraged her to exhibit with them. Cassatt became a mentor to younger American artists and encouraged Americans to buy Impressionist art. She died near Paris in 1926.

♦ IN THE OMNIBUS
This portrait, with its simple lines and lack of shadows, shows the influence of Japanese art on Cassatt's work.

PORTRAIT BY DEGAS
Mary Cassatt in a portrait by Degas. Degas was both a friend and mentor to Cassatt.

WOMAN IN BLACK AT THE OPERA
Cassatt was a close friend of Degas and she shared his interest in the theater. Her focus, however, was not behind the scenes or what was happening on stage. Cassatt was interested in the audience. She painted many scenes of fashionable women attending the opera. In this scene, a woman is absorbed with the action onstage, while a man in another box is busy watching her.

A STUDY ♦
In this painting, Cassatt sought to prove to Degas that gesture and composition were enough to make a beautiful painting, even if the model herself was not a beauty. Degas agreed, and bought the painting himself.

ARMAND GUILLAUMIN

Armand Guillaumin (ghee yoh man) is the least well-known of the Impressionists, even though he regularly exhibited with them and was a member of the group that met at the Café Guerbois. He maintained a lifelong friendship with Camille Pissarro, who introduced him to the other Impressionists and with whom he oftened painted. Guillaumin's work is characterized by vivid colors, bold brushstrokes, and an energy that was unusual for the Impressionist group. His style would influence painters in the twentieth century.

✦ SUNSET AT IVRY
In this work, painted in 1873, Guillaumin displayed his interest in the less beautiful aspects of city life. The intense yellow light of the sunset is reflected on the river.

HIS LIFE
Born in Paris in 1841, Guillaumin did odd jobs during the day so he could take art classes at night. He worked in his uncle's shop, for the railroad, and was a garbage collector for a time. He eventually met Cézanne and Pissarro, and painted with them in the towns surrounding Paris. He took part in several Impressionist exhibitions, including the first one in 1874. He also exhibited at the Salon des Refusés. In 1886, the art dealer Durand-Ruel held an exhibition of his work in New York City. Guillaumin struggled financially until 1891, when he won a lottery, which gave him financial security. He died near Paris in 1927.

✦ SELF-PORTRAIT
Armand Guillaumin in a self-portrait from 1878. He lived longer than any of the other Impressionists, surviving Monet and Cassatt. He did not receive much recognition during his lifetime, but his art has now been rediscovered.

QUAI DE BERCY
Like his fellow Impressionists, Guillaumin shared an interest in landscapes and a fascination with light. The work above, however, painted in 1874, demonstrates some of the differences between his work and that of the other Impressionists. His paintings along the Seine show factory smoke and isolated figures, rather than people enjoying themselves at fashionable resorts. Guillaumin didn't hesitate to use black and other dark tones in his paintings. He contrasted these with bright, often unrealistic, hues. His dynamic use of color inspired the Fauves, a group of twentieth-century painters known for their brilliant colors.

✦ THE SEINE AT PARIS
This work, painted in 1871, was exhibited in the Impressionists' third show. The dark trees contrast with the pale foreground.

GUSTAVE CAILLEBOTTE

Gustave Caillebotte (kye yuh bot) is known for his scenes of city life, though he painted many other subjects as well. His depictions of Paris often focused on its modernity: Haussmann's wide boulevards and elegant new apartment buildings, or the new iron bridges spanning the Seine. Caillebotte was interested in photography and his compositions often featured the type of cropping and asymmetry found in a snapshot. After his paintings were rejected by the Salon, Caillebotte began exhibiting with the Impressionists in 1876.

HIS LIFE
Born in Paris in 1848, to an upper-class family, Caillebotte earned a law degree in 1868. In 1870, he was drafted to fight in the Franco-Prussian War. After the war, he began studying painting. He attended the Impressionists' first exhibition, although he didn't participate in it. His father died in 1874, leaving Caillebotte with a large inheritance. He used much of the money to support his fellow artists, buying their paintings, paying for their studios, and funding many of their exhibitions. When he died in 1894, he left his sizeable collection of Impressionist works to the French government to be displayed in museums.

✦ ROOFTOPS UNDER THE SNOW
Many of Caillebotte's scenes are painted from a high vantage point, including this depiction of Paris rooftops after a snowfall.

✦ MONET RESTING
Caillebotte met Monet in the early 1870s and the two remained close friends. Caillebotte helped Monet financially. While Monet was at Giverny, Caillebotte, who was interested in plants, corresponded with him about gardening.

THE FLOORSCRAPERS
With its dark palette and depiction of people at work, *The Floorscrapers* contains elements of Realism. Caillebotte was breaking new ground, however, by painting city laborers. The Realists painted peasants, but urban workers were a new topic. The painting also reflects Caillebotte's academic training. His brushstrokes are almost imperceptible and the men's bare torsos are reminscent of the idealized bodies in traditional painting. Caillebotte often used exaggerated perspective, but here it is perfectly correct. Despite all of this, the Salon rejected the painting because it considered the subject matter too vulgar.

✦ BOATING
Caillebotte had many hobbies, one of which was building and racing boats. Several of his paintings depict boating on the Yerres River, south of Paris, where his family had an estate.

◆ TIME LINE

1855	First Universal Exposition in Paris, at the Palais de l'Industrie. Camille Pissarro moves to Paris from the Virgin Islands.
1863	The Salon des Refusés opens, with many Impressionist works. Monet meets Bazille, Renoir, and Sisley in Charles Gleyre's studio.
1865	Manet shocks the Salon with *Olympia*. Renoir and Sisley work *en plein air* in the Fontainebleau forest outside of Paris.
1867	Japanese art appears at the Paris Universal Exposition. Impressionists petition the government for another Salon des Refusés.
1869	The artists meet regularly at the Café Guerbois in the Batignolles district. Monet and Renoir paint together at La Grenouillère.
1870	In July, war breaks out between France and Prussia. Monet and Pissarro take shelter in London, where they meet Paul Durand-Ruel.
1871	In January, France and Prussia sign an armistice. The Paris Commune lasts from March 18 until May 28.
1872	Degas visits New Orleans. Pissarro moves to Pointoise. Cassatt exhibits at the Salon for the first time.
1873	Durand-Ruel buys Impressionists' work to exhibit in his London Gallery. Caillebotte's father dies, leaving him a fortune.
1874	The Impressionists' first independent exhibition is held in the studio of photographer Félix Nadar.
1875	The paintings not sold at the 1874 exhibition are auctioned, at very low prices, at the Hôtel Drouot in Paris.
1878	At auction of Ernest Hoschedé's art collection, Impressionist paintings sell for very low prices. Many artists struggle financially.
1881	Sixth Impressionist exhibition. Renoir travels to Algeria and Italy. Manet is proposed for the Legion of Honor.
1882	Seventh Impressionist exhibition. A great retrospective exhibition of Courbet is held in Paris.
1883	Durand-Ruel hosts shows for Monet, Renoir, Sisley, and Pissarro and organizes exhibits in London and Berlin. Manet dies at age fifty-one.
1884	Commemorative exhibition of Manet at the École des Beaux-Arts. Monet paints with Renoir in Italy.
1885	Pissarro meets Pointillist painter Seurat. Monet exhibit hosted by Georges Petit, an art dealer and rival of Durand-Ruel.
1886	Impressionists' eighth and final joint exhibition. Durand-Ruel holds major exhibition of Impressionist works in New York. The group disbands.

◆ GLOSSARY

armistice: an agreement to suspend hostilities prior to the signing of a peace treaty

asymmetrical: in a painting, arranging objects so that they are not balanced, in terms of size and form, on opposite sides of a central, imaginary line

composition: the way in which the elements in an artwork are arranged

contemporaries: individuals who are living in the same time period

cropped: cut off at the edge of a page or frame

Cubism: an art movement of the early twentieth century in which objects are broken up and reassembled so that they can be viewed from multiple angles

en plein air: a French phrase meaning "in the open air." In art, it refers to painting outdoors.

Expressionism: an art movement at the beginning of the twentieth century that uses exaggerated color or distorted forms for an emotional effect

foreground: the part of a picture that is closest to the viewer

satire: a piece of art or writing that aims to ridicule

WEB SITES

Experience Impressionism
www.impressionism.org
A guided tour through the history of Impressionism. Includes analyses of individual works and artist biographies.

Manet and the Railway
www.nga.gov/collection/railwel.shtm
An illustrated guide to Impressionism from the National Gallery of Art.

Impressionism and Post-Impressionism
www.artic.edu/artaccess/AA_Impressionist/
An overview of the artists and their works. Includes maps, glossary, and pronunciation guide.

♦ LIST OF WORKS INCLUDED IN THIS BOOK

The works reproduced in this book are listed below, with their date, when known, the museum or gallery where they are currently held, and the number of the page on which they appear. Where no gallery is shown, the work is in a private collection. The numbers in bold type refer to the credits on page 64, which give further information about some of the works.. The works are listed in alphabetical order by the artist.

Abbreviations:

w = whole; D = detail

BFA: Boston, Museum of Fine Arts; CFM: Cambridge, Fitzwilliam Museum; NMW: Cardiff, National Museum of Wales; CAI: Chicago, Art Institute; CG: London, Courtauld Institute Galleries; NG: London, National Gallery; NYM: New York, Metropolitan Museum of Art; MOMA: New York, Museum of Modem Art; BN: Paris, Bibliothèque Nationale; MM: Paris, Musée Marmottan; MO: Paris, Musée d'Orsay; PMA: Philadelphia, Museum of Art; WNG: Washington, D.C., National Gallery of Art.

BAZILLE, FRÉDÉRIC

1 *Bathers* 1869 (Cambridge, Mass., Harvard University, Fogg Art Museum) 28 w; **2** *Landscape at Chailly* 1865 (CAI, Charles H. and Mary F.S. Worchester Coll.) 17 w.

CABANEL, ALEXANDRE

3 *The Birth of Venus* 1863 (MO) 45 w.

CAILLEBOTTE, GUSTAVE

4 *The Floorscrapers* 1875 (MO) 27 D, 61 w; **5** *The Man at the Window* 1876 9 D; **6** *Monet Resting* 1884 (Geneva, Musée du Petit Palais) 61 D; **7** *Canoes* 1878 (Musée des Beaux -Arts, Rennes) 61 D; **8** *Paris, A Rainy Day* 1876-77 (CAI, Charles H. and Mary F.S. Worchester Coll.) 39 w; **9** *Rooftops under the Snow* 1878 (MO) 61 w; **10** *Self-Portrait* c. 1889 (MO) 27 D.

CASSATT, MARY

11 *The Child's Bath* (CAI, Robert A Waller Fund) 1891-92 59 w; **12** *Girl Arranging Her Hair* 1886 (WNG, Chester Dale Coll.) 59 w; **13** *The Hairstyle* 1891 (CAI, Mr. and Mrs. Potter Palmer Coll.) 23 w; **14** *In the Omnibus* c.1891 (WNG, Chester Dale Coll.) 59 w; **15** *Lady at the Tea Table* 1885 (NYM) 27 D; **16** *Woman Bathing* 1891 (BN) 23 w; **17** *Woman in Black at the Opéra* 1880 (BFA, Hayden Coll.) 59 w.

CÉZANNE, PAUL

18 *The Card Players* 1898 (MO) 55 w; **19** *The House of the Hanged Man* 1873-74 (MO) 37 w; **20** *House on a Hill* 1904-6 (WNG) 45 w; **21** *The Large Bathers* 1900-5 (PMA, Purchased: W.P. Wilatach Coll.) 27 D, 55 w; **22** *Mont Sainte-Victoire* 1900-02 (Paris, Louvre, cabinet des dessins) 54 w; **23** *Mont Sainte-Victoire viewed from Les Lauves* 1904-06 (PMA) 54 w; **24** *Mont Sainte-Victoire viewed from the Bibemus quarry* c.1897 (Baltimore, Museum of Art, The Cone Coll., formed by Dr. Claribel Cone and Mrs. Etta Cone) 54-55 w; **25** *Portrait of Victor Choquet* c.1877 (Richmond, Virginia Museum of Fine Arts, Mr. and Mrs. Paul Mellon Coll.) 41 D; **26** *The Seine at Beny* 1876 (Hamburg, Kunsthalle) 18 w; **27** *Self-Portrait* 1881 (Munich, Neue Pinakothek) 27 w; **28** *Still Life with Apples and Biscuits* 1879-82 (MO) 19 D; **29** *Still Life with Apples and Peaches* 1905 (WNG, gift of Eugene and Agnes E. Meyer) 55 w; **30** *Wood in Provence* c.1888 (NMW) 19 D.

COROT, JEAN BAPTISTE CAMILLE

31 *View of Ville d'Avray* (Paris, Louvre) 15 w.

COURBET, GUSTAVE

32 *The Burial at Ornans* 1849-50 (MO) 15 w; **33** *The Painter's Studio, a real allegory...* 1855 (MO) 14 w.

COUTURE, THOMAS

34 *The Romans of the Decadence* 1847 (MO) 13 w.

DAUMIER, HONORÉ

35 *The battle between realism and classical idealism* 1855 ("Le Charivari") 14.

DEGAS, EDGAR

36 *Absinthe* 1874 (MO) 53 w; **37** *Getting out of the bath* 1876-77 (MO) 53 w; **38** *After the Bath – Woman Drying Herself* 1896 (PMA) 25 w; **39** *At the Races* 1876-77 (MO) 33 D; **40** *At the Stock Exchange* c.1878-79 (MO) 27 D; **41** sketch of Ingres's *The Bather* c. 1855 (BN) 10 w; **42** *The Bellelli Family* 1858-67 (MO) 26 D; **43** *Café-concert* 1877 (Lyon, Musée des Beaux-Arts) 33 D; **44** *Carriage at the Races* 1870-72 (BFA) 37 w; **45** *The Cotton Exchange, New Orleans* 1873 (Pau, Musée des Beaux-Arts) 26 D; **46** *The Gentlemen's Race - Before the Start* 1862 (MO) 32 D; **47** *Hortense Valpinçon* 1871 (Minneapolis, Institute of Arts) 26 D; **48** *In the Omnibus* 1877-78 (Paris, Musée Picasso) 52 w; **49** *Little Fourteen-Year-Old Dancer* 1879-81 (Vermont, Shelburne Museum) 52 w; **50** *Nude study for the Little Fourteen-Year-Old Dancer* 1881 (Christie's, London) 52 w; **51** *Place de la Concorde* 1875 6 D ; **52** *Portrait of Mary Cassatt* c.1884 (Washington, Smithsonian Institution) 59 D; **53** *Racehorses in front of the Stands* c.1866-68 (MO) 32 D; **54** *The Rehearsal of the Ballet on Stage* c.1874 (NYM) 52-53 w; **55** *Self-Portrait* 1854-55 (MO) 27 w; **56** *The Star* 1876-77 (MO) 33 D; **57** *The Tub* 1886 (MO) 27 D; **58** *A Woman Ironing* 1873 (NYM) 26 D; 59 *Women Ironing* 1884-86 (MO) 53 w; **60** *Women on a Café Terrace* 1877 (MO) 32 D.

DELACROIX, EUGÈNE

61 *Liberty Leading the People* 1830 (Paris, Louvre) 44 w.

FANTIN-LATOUR, HENRI DE

62 *Studio in the Batignolles District* 1870 (MO) 31 w.

GAUGUIN, PAUL

63 *The Beach at Dieppe* 1885 (Copenhagen, Ny Carlsberg Glyptothek) 45 w.

GLEYRE, CHARLES

64 *Lost Illusions* 1851 (Paris, Louvre) 13 w.

GUILLAUMIN, ARMAND

65 *The Bridge of Louis Philippe* 1875 (WNG, Chester Dale Coll.) 7 w; **66** *Quai de Bercy* 1874 (Paris, Musée Carnavalet) 60 w; **67** *The Seine at Charenton* 1878 (MO) 19 w; **68** *The Seine at Paris* 1871 (Houston, Museum of Fine Arts, The John A. and Audrey Jones Coll.) 60 w; **69** *Self-Portrait* 1878 (Amsterdam, Van Gogh Museum) 60 D; **70** *Sunset at Ivry* 1873 (MO) 60 w.

HOKUSAI

71 *Self-Portrait* 1842 (Leiden, Rijksmuseum voor Volkenkunde) 22 w.

INGRES, JEAN AUGUSTE DOMINIQUE

72 *The Bather of Valpinçon* 1808 (Paris, Louvre) 10 w; **73** *Le Bain Turc* 1859-63 (Paris, Louvre) 45 w.

KUNIYOSHI

74 *Fan* 1848 (London, British Museum) 22 w.

MANET, ÉDOUARD

75 *The Absinthe Drinker* 1858-59 (Copenhagen, Ny Carlsberg Glyptothek) 47 w; **76** *The Balcony* 1868-69 (MO) 27 D; **77** *A Bar at the Folies-Bergère* 1881-82 (CG) 33 D; **78** *The Barricade* 1871 (Budapest, Szépnuïveszeti Museum) 35 D; **79** *The Battle of the Kearsage and the Alabama* 1864 (PMA, John G. Johnson Coll.) 47 w; **80** *The Beer Waitress* 1877-79 (MO) 26 D; **81** *Berthe Morisot in a Black Hat, with a Bunch of Violets* 1872 27 D, 58 D; **82** *Boy Blowing Soap Bubbles* 1867 (Lisbon, Calouste Gulbenkian Foundation) 26 D; **83** *Chez Père Lathuille* 1879 (Tournai, Musée des Beaux-Arts) 32 D; **84** *Luncheon on the grass* 1863 (MO) 21 w, 46-47 w; **85** *The Fifer* 1866 (MO) 26 D; **86** *Horse Racing at Longchamps* c.1867 (CAI, Mr. and Mrs. Potter Palmer Coll.) 32 D; **87** *Mlle Victorine in the Costume of an Espada* 1862 (NYM) 47 w; **88** *Masked Ball at the Opéra* 1873-74 (WNG, gift of Mrs. Horace Havemayer in memory of her mother-in-law, Louisine Havemeyer) 33 D; **89** *Monet in his Floating Studio* 1874 (Munich, Neue Pinakothek) 17 w, **90** *Music in the Tuileries Gardens* 1862 (NG) 47 D; **91** *Olympia* 1863 (MO) 21 w; **92** *Rockefort's Escape* 1881 (Zurich, Kunsthaus) 18 D; **93** *Roses and Tulips in a Dragon Vase* c.1882 19 D; **94** *Café* 1869 (Cambridge, Mass., Harvard University, Fogg Art Museum) 31 D.

MATISSE, HENRI

95 *Luxe, Calme et Volupté* 1904-5 (MO) 44 w.

MILLET, JEAN FRANÇOIS

96 *The Gleaners* 1857 (MO) 15 w.

MONET, CLAUDE

97 *The Artist's Garden at Giverny* 1900 (MO) 16 w; **98** *The Artist's House at Argenteuil* 1873 (CAI, Mr. and Mrs. Martin A. Ryerson Coll.) 44 w; **99** *Boulevard des Capucines* 1873-74 (Kansas City, The Nelson-Atkins Museum of Art) 7 w, 38 D; **100** *Boulevard des Capucines* 1873 (Moscow, Pushkin Museum) 37 D; **101** *Cliffs at Etretat* 885 (MM) 16 w; **102** *Cliff Walk at Pourville* 1882 (CAI, Mr. and Mrs. Lewis Lamed Coburn Memorial Coll.) 17 w; 103 *Forest of Fontainebleau* 1864 (MO) 17 w; **104** *Gare Saint-Lazare* 1877 (MO) 7 w; **105** *La Grenouillère* 1869 (ONM) 28-29 w; **106** *Haystacks, end of summer* 1890-91 (MO) 4849 w; **107** *Impression: Sunrise* 1872 (MM) 36 w; **108** *The Japanese Bridge in Giverny* 1900 (CAI, Mr. and Mrs. Lewis Lamed Coburn Memorial Coll.) 23 w; **109** *La Japonaise* 1876 (BFA) 23 D; **110** *Jardin de l'Infante* 1866 (Oberlin College, Ohio, Allen Memorial Art Museum, R.T. Miller, Jr Fund, 1948) 38 D; **111** *Lemon Trees at Bordighera* 1884 (Copenhagen, Ny Carlsberg Glyptothek) 49 w,, **112** *The Magpie* 1868-69 (MO) 19 D; **113** *Pont de l'Europe* 1877 (MM) 6 w; **114** *Poplars* 1891 (NYM) 19 D; **115** *Quai du Louvre* 1867 (The Hague, Haags Gemeentemuseum) 7 w, 38 D; **116** *Regatta at Argenteuil* 1872 (MO) 49 w; **117** *Rouen Cathedral, sun effect, late in the day* 1892-94 (MM) 42 D; **118** *Rouen Cathedral, the portal* 1892-94 (WNG, Chester Dale Coll) 43 D; **119** *Rouen Cathedral, the portal* 1892-94 (Moscow, Pushkin Museum) 43 D; **120** *Rouen Cathedral, symphony in grey and pink* 1892-94 (NMW) 42 D; **121** *Rouen, Cathedral The portal, harmony in blue* 1892-94 (MO) 42 D; **122** *Rouen Cathedral The portal, harmony in blue and gold, bright sun* 1892-94 (MO) 42 D; **123** *[Rouen; Cathedral] The portal, harmony in grey, dull weather* 1892,94 (MO) 43 D; **124** *[Rouen Cathedral] The portal, morning effect* 1892-94 (Basel, Galerie Beyeler) 42 D; **125** *[Rouen Cathedral] The portal and Alban Tower, dawn* 1892-94 (BFA) 43 D; **126** *[Rouen Cathedral] The portal and Alban Tower, harmony in white* 1892-94 (MO) 43 D; **127** *[Rouen Cathedral] The portal and Alban Tower, dull weather* 1892-94 (Rouen, Musée des Beaux-Arts) 43 D; **128** *[Rouen Cathedral] The portal, morning fog* 1892-94 (Essen, Folkwang Museum) 42 D; **129** *[Rouen Cathedral] The portal, midday* 1892-94 (Williamstown, Mass., Sterling and Francine Clark Institute) 43 D; **130** *[Rouen Cathedral] The portal, sunshine* 1892-94 (Moscow, Pushkin Museum) 42 D; **131** *[Rouen Cathedral] The Portal, sunshine* 1892-94 (WNG, Chester Dale Coll.) 43 D; **132** *[Rouen Cathedral] The portal, harmony in brown* 1892-94 (MO) 42 D; **133** *Rue Montorgeuil Decked Out with Flags* 1878 (MO) 39 D; **134** *The Seine at Argenteuil* 1873 (CG) 17 w; **135** *The Station at Argenteuil* c. 1872 (Pontoise, Musée Pissarro) 17 w; **136** *Terrace at Saint-Adresse* 1867 NM 16 w, 19 D; **137** *Les Tuileries* 1876 (MM) 7 w; **138** *Vétheuil in Summer* 1879 (Toronto, Art Gallery of Ontario) 49 w; **139** *Vétheuil in Winter* 1879 (New York, Frick Collection) 49,w, **140** *Waterlilies* 1908 (MO) 49 D.

MORISOT, BERTHE

141 *The Cradle* 1873 (MO) 37 w; **142** *The Harbour of Lorient* 1869 (WNG, Ailsa Mellon Bruce Coll.) 58 w; **143** *The Quay at Bougival* 1883 (Oslo, Nasjonalgalleriet) 17 w, 58 w; **144** *The Mother and Sister of the Artist* 1870 (WNG, Chester Dale Coll.) 58 w; **145** *Woman at Her Toilette* c.1875 (CAI, Stilmey Fund) 58 w.

MUNCH, EDVARD

146 *Rue Lafayette* 1891 (Bergen, Museo Storico) 45 w. PICASSO, PABLO

147 *Les Demoiselles d'Avignon* 1907 (MOMA, acquired through the Lillie P. Bliss Bequest) 45 w.

PISSARRO, CAMILLE

148 *Avenue de l'Opéra* 1898 (Reims, Musée des Beaux-Arts) 7 w, **149** *The Backwoods at l'Hermitage* 1879 (Cleveland, Museum of Art, gift of the Hanna Fund) 56 w; **150** *Boieldieu Bridge, Rouen, at sunset* 1896 (Birmingham, Museum and Art Gallery) 39 w; **151** *Boulevard des Italiens* 1897 (WNG, Chester Dale Coll.) 7 w, **152** *Boulevard Montmartre* 1897 (London, Cristie's) 39 D; **153** *Factory near Pontoise* 1873 (Springfield, Museum of Fine Arts, James Philip Gray Coll.) 56 w; **154** *February, Sunrise* 1893 (Otterlo, Kröller-Müller Museum) 18 D; **155** *Hoarfrost* 1878 (MO) 37 w; **156** *The Pork Butcher* 1883 (London, Tate Gallery) 26 D; **157** *The Road, Louveciennes* 1872 (MO) 17 w; **158** *Rue de l'Epicerie, Rouen* 1898 (NYM) 16 w; **159** *The Seine at Marly* 1872 (Stuttgart, Staatsgalerie) 17 w; **160** *View of Pontoise* 1876 (Paris, Musée du Petit Palais) 17 w; **161** *Young Woman Washing Dishes* 1882 (CFM) 56 w.

RAIMONDI, MARCANTONIO

162 *The Judgment of Paris* 1515-16 (NYM) 46 D.

RENOIR, PIERRE-AUGUSTE

163 *Arab Festival* 1881 (MO) 51 w; **164** *At the Inn of Mother Anthony* 1866 (Stockhohn, Statens Konstmuseer) 33 D; **165** *The Bathers* 1918-19 (MO) 50 w; **166** *The Boating Party* 1880-81 (Washington, Phillips Collection) 32 D; **167** *The Box at the Opéra* 1874 (CG) 37 w; **168** *The Children's Afternoon at Wargemont* 1884 (Berlin, Bildarchiv Preusischer Kulturbesitz) 26 D; **169** *Claude Monet Reading* 1872 (MM) 27 D; **170** *A Dance in the City* 1872-73 (MO) 33 D; **171** *A Dance in the Country* 1872-73 (MO) 33 D; **172** *The Garden of the Rue Cortot* 1876 (Pittsburgh, The CarnegieMuseum of Art) 51 w; **173** *The Great Bathers* 1884-87 (PMA, Mr. and Mrs. Carroll S. Tyson Coll.) 50 w; **174** *La Grenouillère* 1869 (Stockholm, Statens Konstmuseer) 29 w, **175** *Gust of Wind* c.1872 (CFM) 18 D; **176** *M et Mme Bernheim de Villers* 1910 (MO) 27 D; **177** *Dance at the Moulin de la Galette* 1876 (MO) 7 w, 33 D, 50-51 w; **178** *Nana* 1876 (Moscow, Pushkin Museum) 27 D; **179** *Nude in the Sunlight* 1875 (MO) 27 D; **180** *Path Climbing Through Long Grass* 1874 (MO) 18 D; **181** *Place Clichy* 1880 (CFM) 39 D; **182** *Pont Neuf* 1872 (WNG, Ailsa Mellon Bruce Coll.) 39 D; **183** *Portrait of Bazille* 1867 (MO) 35 w; **184** *Sailboats at Argenteuil* 1874 (Portland, Museum of Art) 51 w; **185** *Skaters in the Bois de Boulogne* 1868, 6 w; **186** *Young Woman Sewing* 1879 (CAI, Mr. and Mrs. Lewis Lamed Coburn Memorial Coll.) 26 D.

SEURAT, GEORGES

187 *Sunday Afternoon on the Island of La Grande Jatte* 1884-86 (CAI, Helen Birch Bartlett Memorial Coll.) 44 w.

SISLEY, ALFRED

188 *Boats on the Seine* (CG) 57 w; **189** *Floods at Port-Marly* 1876 (MO) 57 w; **190** *Rue de la Machine, Louveciennes* 1873 (MO) 57 w; **191** *Snow at Louveciennes* 1874 (Washington, Phillips Collection) 17 w; **192** *View of Montmartre* 1869 (Grenoble, Musée) 7 w; **193** Wheatfields near Argenteuil 1873 (Hamburg, Kunsthalle). 18 w.

TOULOUSE-LAUTREC, HENRI DE

194 *At the Moulin Rouge* 1892 (CAI, Helen Birch Bartlett Memorial Coll.) 45 w; **195** *La Goulue* 189132 w.

VAN GOGH, VINCENT

196 *Wheatfield with Crows* 1890 (Amsterdam, Van Gogh Museum) 45 w.

♦ INDEX

♦ CREDITS

The original and previously unpublished illustrations in this book may only be reproduced with the prior permission of Donati-Giudici Associati, who holds the copyright.

The illustrations are by: L.R. Galante (pages 4-5, 10-11, 12-13, 20-21, 22-23, 24-25, 28-29, 30-31, 40-41); Andrea Ricciardi (pages 6-7, 8-9, 16-17, 34-35); Claudia Saraceni (pages 14, 38).

All efforts have been made to trace the copyright holders of the other illustrations in the book. If any omissions have been made, this will be corrected at reprint.

Thanks are due to the following for their permission to use illustrations: Allen Memorial Art Museum, Oberlin; Art Gallery of Ontario, Toronto; The Art Institute of Chicago; Bibillothèque Nationale, Paris; British Museum, London; Monsieur C. Blifirle, Zurich; The Carnegie Museum of Art, Pittsburgh; Courtauld Institute Galleries, London; Fitzwilliam Museum, Cambridge; Fogg Art Museum, Cambridge, Mass., Harvard University, Folkwang Museum, Essen; Frick Collection, New York, Galerie Bayeler, Basel; Grenoble Museum; Calouste Gulbenkian Foundation, Lisbon; Haags Gemeentemuseum, The Hague, Institute of Arts, Minneapolis; Kunsthalle, Hamburg, Kunsthaus, Zurich; Metropolitan Museum of Art, New York, Musée des Beaux-Arts, Lyon; Musée des Beaux-Arts, Pau; Musée des Beaux-Arts, Reims; Musée des Beaux-Arts, Rouen; Musée des Beaux-Arts, Tournai; Musée Carnavalet, Paris; Musée d'Orsay, Paris, Musée du Louvre, Paris, Musée du Petit Palais, Geneva; Musée du Petit Palais, Paris; Musée Marmottan, Paris; Musée Municipale A.G. Poulain, Vernon; Musée Picasso, Paris; Musée Pissarro, Pontoise; Museum and Art Gallery, Birmingham; Museum of Art Baltimore; Museum of Art Cleveland; Museum of Art, Portland, Museum of Fine Arts, Boston; Museum of Fine Arts, Houston, Museum of Fine Arts, Springfield; Museum of Modem Art, New York, Nasjonalgalleriet, Oslo; National Gallery, London; National Gallery of Art Washington, D.C.; National Museum of Wales, Cardiff; National Museum Vincent Van Gogh, Amsterdam, The Nelson Atkins Museum of Art, Kansas City; Neue Pinakothek, Munich; Ny Carlsberg Glyptothek, Copenhagen; Philadelphia Museum of Art Phillips Collection, Washington, D.C.; Pushkin Museum, Moscow, Rijksmuseum Kröller Müller, Otterlo; Rijksmuseum voor Volkenkunde, Leiden; Shelburne Museum, Vermont; Smithsonian Institution, Washington, D.C.; Staatsgalerie, Stuttgart; Statens Konstmuseer, Stockholm; Sterling and Francine Clark Institute, Willliamstown, Mass.; Szépnuíveszeti Museum, Budapest; The Tate Gallery, London; Virginia Museum of Fine Arts, Richmond.
ARCHIVIO ALINARI/GIRAUDON: 3, 7, 9, 10, 28, 33, 40, 42, 45, 46, 50, 55, 56, 57, 60, 62, 67, 70, 77, 80, 81, 90, 92, 95, 97, 103, 104, 106, 107, 112, 113, 121, 122, 123, 126, 127, 133, 137, 148, 152, 155, 157, 163, 169, 170, 171, 176, 189, 190; BRIDGEMAN/ARTEPHOTO: 119, 130, 185; PHOTO SCALA, FLORENCE 4, 18, 19, 22, 27, 32, 34, 36, 39, 41, 53, 59, 61, 72, 73, 74, 76, 83, 84, 85, 89, 91, 96, 116, 132, 141, 146, 165, 167, 177, 179, 180,183; © PHOTO R.M.N.: 31, 37, 48, 64, 140; PHOTO BASSET. 42; BILDARCHIV PREUSISCHER KULTURBESITZ, BERLIN, PHOTO JÖRG P. ANDERS: 168; 2 © 1994 CAI, oil on canvas, 81.5 x 101.6 cm; 8 0 1994 CAI, oil on canvas 212.2 x 276.2 cm; 11 © 1994 CAI, oil on canvas; 12 WNG, 1994 Board of Trustees, oil on canvas, 75.1 x 62.5, 13 © 1994 Arc, etching, 4.3 x 29.9 cm; 14 WNG, 1994 Board of Trustees, soft ground etching, drypoint and aquatint in color, 15 © 1994 NYM; 17 Courtesy HFA, oil on canvas, 80 x 64.8; 20 cm Presented by the U.S. Government in memory of Charles A. Loeser, on loan to the WNG, tela, 65.8 x 81 on; 21 Purchased: W.P., Wilatach Cot; 29 WNG, 1994 Board of Trustees, oil on canvas, 81 x 100.5 cm, 38 Purchased: Estate of the Late George D. Widener; 44 Courtesy BFA, 1931 Purchase Fund, oil on canvas, 36.5 x 55.9 cm; 54 © 1994 NYM; 65 WNG, 1994 Board of Trustees, oil on canvas, 45.8 x 60.5 cm, 86 © 1994 CAI, oil on canvas, 43.9 x 84.5 m. 87 © 1994 Nym; 88 WNG, 1994 Board of Trustees, oil on canvas, 59 x 72.5 cm; 98 © 1994 CAI, oil on canvas, 43.9 x 84.5 cm; 99 Purchased: The Kenneth A. and Helen Spencer Foundation Acquisition Fund, oil on canvas, 80.4 x 60.3 cm; 101© MM; 102 © 1994 CAI, oil on canvas, 66.5 x 82.3 cm; 105 © 1994 NYM; 108 © 1994 CAI, oil on canvas, 89.9 x 101; 109 cm Courtesy BFA, 1951 Purchase Fund, oil on canvas, 231.6 x 142.3 cm, 114 © 1994 NYM, 117 © mm; 118 WNG, 1994 Board of Trustees, oil on canvas, 100.4 x 66; 125 cm Courtesy BFA, 1951 Purchase Fund, oil on canvas, 231.6 x 142.3 cm; 131 WNG, 1994 Board of Trustees, oil on canvas; 136 © 1994 NYM; 139 © THE FRICK COLL., NEW YORK 142 WNG, 1994 Board of Trustees, oil on canvas, 101 x 81.8 cm; 144 WNG, 1994 Board of Trustees, oil on canvas; 145 © 1994 CAI, oil on canvas, 60.3 x 80.4 cm; 147 oil on canvas, 243.9 x 233.7 cm; 149 oil on canvas, 125.1 x 163.2 cm, 151 WNG, 1994 Board of Trustees, oil on canvas, 73.2 x 92.1 cm; 158 © 1994 Hym; 162 © 1994 Nym; 166 © THE PHILLIPS COLL., WASHINGTON, D.C.; 172 Acquired through the generosity of Mrs. Alan M. Scaife, oil on canvas, 151.8 x 97.5 cm; 182 WNG, 1994 Board of Trustees, oil on canvas, 75.3 x 93.7 cm; 186 © 1994 CAI, oil on canvas, 61.5 x 50.3 cm; 187 © 1994 CAI, oil on canvas, 123 x 141 cm; 1910 THE PHILLIPS COLL., WASHINGTON, D.C.; 194 © 1994 CAI, oil on canvas, 123 x 141 cm. The paintings of Edvard Munch, Henri Matisse and Pablo Picasso on pages 44-45 have been reproduced with the authorization of the Società italiana degli autori ed editori, which has agreed to deal with any concerns about rights.